Richard M. Spielmann

HISTORY
OF
CHRISTIAN
WORSHIP

THE SEABURY PRESS
NEW YORK

To Janet

Preface

THIS BOOK has evolved from two major concerns. During the past few years, I have had opportunity to speak to various groups of laity and clergy about some aspects of the history and theology of Christian worship. Invariably members of these groups have asked me to suggest books, usually of a popular and nontechnical nature, for their reading in the subject. This has been somewhat difficult to do because most of the historical studies of Christian worship are rather scholarly and lengthy works, or at least technical enough to assume a good deal of background on the reader's part. The few more popular books on the subject have usually encompassed an apologia for worship and an explanation or rationale of the Church's services with little emphasis on the history of worship. In this book, therefore, I have sought to produce a general history of Christian worship, which I hope is sufficiently nontechnical to be read profitably by laymen and clergymen.

Another of my major concerns has been liturgical renewal, an exciting cause which has affected most Christian churches, especially in the past two decades. Many excellent books, including some popular and easily readable ones, have been written on liturgical renewal and the liturgical movement. A problem, however, that appears in many of these books is that the authors, for various reasons, have had to assume a general knowledge of the history of Christian worship on the part of the readers. Yet all too often the readers unfortunately have not had opportunity to gain this historical background. Thus, this book has also been written to provide historical perspective for the Church's concern about liturgical renewal. At this time such a historical perspective seems to be necessary if liturgical renewal is to be more widely accepted in all Christian churches.

I should also like to direct the reader to the bibliography at the back of the book. This is a *general* history of worship that seeks to cover the main issues of the subject from biblical times to the present day. Hopefully such a general history will cause the reader to pursue the subject, either as a whole or in special areas, through further reading. This is the main point of the type of bibliography that I have provided. Also, because the nature of the book precluded the use of footnotes, the bibliography will provide the more critical reader with some of the secondary sources consulted by the author.

Any author is profoundly grateful to the many people who aid him in the writing and publishing of a book. In addition to the staff of the Seabury Press, which has been so helpful to me, I should like to cite four people to whom I am especially thankful. Two who have been indirectly involved in this book are Professor Powel M. Dawley, of The

General Theological Seminary in New York, who first inspired me in the ways of church history; and Professor Cyril
C. Richardson, of Union Theological Seminary in New York,
who gave me my grounding in the study of liturgy.

With respect to the book, I am deeply grateful to my
colleague at Bexley Hall, the Reverend Robert J. Page, who
read the entire manuscript and made many valuable suggestions. Finally my deepest appreciation goes to my wife,
to whom the book is dedicated. In typing the book from
original manuscript to final draft, she has made some very
helpful suggestions concerning language and style. More
important to me, though, than typing and suggestions have
been her enthusiasm for the book and her encouragement of
me in writing it.

R.M.S.

Whit Tuesday, 1966

Contents

Contents

Introduction

PATTERNS OF WORSHIP in Christian churches have been changing rapidly in the past few years. Within all churches there have been pleas for liturgical renewal; and a growing number of clergy and laity have become involved, even caught up, in what is called the liturgical movement. But what is this liturgical movement, and why are Christians being called to liturgical renewal? Perhaps the clearest answers to these questions are revealed by looking first at the signs of liturgical renewal which already exist and then by discussing the causes which produced them.

In the past few decades, many American Protestant churches, such as the Lutheran, Methodist, Presbyterian, and Evangelical United Brethren, have issued new service books or revised forms for public worship. Denominational organizations such as the Methodist Order of St. Luke and the Lutheran Institute for Liturgical Studies at Valparaiso

University have been studying and promoting the principle of liturgical renewal within American Protestantism. The Faith and Order Commission of the World Council of Churches has done much to stimulate interest in and study of the corporate worship of world-wide Protestantism.

Roman Catholics are experiencing radical alterations in their worship because of the work of the recent Vatican Council and the decrees of Pope Paul VI. Much of the Sunday Mass is no longer in Latin but in the language of the people. The congregation is singing hymns and other parts of the service and is being called into greater participation in the Mass. The priest often celebrates from the east side of the altar facing the people, and sermons are preached at all Sunday Masses. Through coverage by newspapers, magazines, and television, as well as from conversations with Roman Catholic friends, the many exciting changes in Roman Catholic worship have become familiar to Christians throughout the world. Perhaps the greatest stimulus in recent years to Protestant liturgical reform and renewal has come from the communication media's coverage of the Vatican Council and of liturgical renewal in the Roman Catholic Church.

The world-wide Anglican Communion, with its traditional Catholic nature and Protestant heritage, has contributed to, and been influenced by, Protestant and Catholic liturgical movements. Through individuals and small groups of bishops, priests, and laymen, but especially through the work of the Associated Parishes in the American Episcopal Church and the Parish and People movement in the Church of England, many liturgical changes have permeated Anglican churches in the past few decades. The emphasis upon the Eucharist, or Holy Communion, as the main Sunday service, the increased involvement of the laity in the services, the revival of a congregational type of church music, and an emphasis on the reading and interpretative preaching of

Holy Scripture are some of the elements which have affected public worship in Episcopal and Anglican churches.

Liturgical renewal throughout Christendom has precipitated change. Sometimes it has been radical change; often it has been minor change. Yet in man's history any change, by its very nature, seems to create some confusion, lack of understanding, and even hostility. The liturgical movement has not been spared these problems. Christian people, Protestant and Catholic, are asking honest and sincere questions: Why the change? What is the liturgical movement seeking to do?

The chief purpose of the twentieth-century liturgical movement has always been to restore corporate worship as central and essential to Christianity, the Church, and the Christian life. The key words here are "restore" and "essential." For in the Christian Church of New Testament times, and especially in the early centuries of Christianity, the corporate worship of the Christian community was central and essential.

The proclamation of the liturgical movement speaks urgently to both Catholic and Protestant Christianity. Since the Reformation of the sixteenth century, the primary doctrine of Protestantism has been faith in God through Christ; that is, man becomes righteous and acceptable to God by virtue of his faith in Christ. But the Protestant advocates of liturgical renewal quickly add that the corporate worship of the Christian community is the Christian's chief response to faith. Faith leads to worship; worship is the response to faith. Furthermore, in actual experience, corporate worship often stimulates faith; faith is broadened and deepened through the common worship of the community of believers.

The central element in Catholic Christianity has always been the Church. Yet the Catholic liturgical movement has had to remind Catholic Christians that in the Church's tra-

ditional doctrine, the primary act or work of the Church is
the offering of corporate worship through Christ to the
Father. The Church is being the Church, in the fullest sense,
when she is worshiping God through the corporate liturgy.
Therefore, whether one's approach to Christianity is Catholic
or Protestant, the corporate worship of the Christian community must be basic and essential.

At this point some would state that all this is readily acceptable, so why the emphasis upon liturgical renewal with
its resultant changes in patterns of worship? The Protestant
or Catholic exponents of the liturgical movement would reply that the centrality of corporate worship is only theoretically accepted in Western Christianity. In actual practice,
Catholic and Protestant churches have not allowed corporate
worship to hold a central place in Christianity. No Protestant
would deny the importance of corporate worship; yet until
recently many Protestant churches did not hold Sunday services during the summer months. Even today most Protestant
congregations have less, sometimes considerably less, than
50 per cent of their membership present at the Sunday offering of corporate worship.

The Roman Catholic Church has a somewhat better per-
centage of the faithful at Sunday worship, for attendance at
Sunday Mass is obligatory. Actually, however, much of the
thrust behind liturgical renewal in this century has come
from the Roman Church, chiefly because so many baptized
Roman Catholics were not at Mass on Sunday. During the
past twenty years, a great deal of the impetus of the liturgical movement has come from French Roman Catholics.
The reason for this clearly lies in the fact that France's
population is over 90 per cent Roman Catholic, yet participation in corporate worship is far less on the average.

The task of the liturgical movement, then, is to restore
and renew corporate worship throughout the churches in

order that worship will resume its centrality in Christianity. In many ways this task involves history, for the major premise of liturgical renewal is that in biblical and early church Christianity, corporate worship was a basic and essential element. Moreover, in order to deal with this task the proponents of liturgical renewal have had to understand first the reasons for the decline of corporate worship. These reasons also involve history.

Perhaps the strangest disclosure to come out of Catholic and Protestant liturgical renewal has been that the two chief causes of the decline of corporate worship are the same for Catholics and Protestants. Briefly, these are excessive individualism and the lack, even prohibition, of congregational involvement in corporate worship. Protestant individualism began to develop in the Reformation and became a central feature of seventeenth- to twentieth-century Protestantism. The Protestant message declared that the purpose of Christianity was to establish a personal faith relationship between the individual and God. The Gospel of Christ should lead the individual to a personal encounter with God, the fruit of which would be moral actions and charitable works in this life and salvation in the life to come. In the midst of all this, the corporate worship of the Christian community had little importance, except perhaps as a means of preparation for the personal encounter between God and the individual. The unimportance of corporate worship was borne out in actual practice. The Sunday service in most Protestant churches revolved around an individual: the minister. He read the Bible, preached at length upon biblical texts, and prayed—sometimes at great length—in order that the individual hearers in the congregation would be led to a personal faith relationship with God and to a moral life in the world. In this Sunday meeting, called the Preaching Service, the Christian community did not offer its worship to God; in reality

the members of the congregation were spectators—hearers
—who came to be edified and stirred up. For many Protestants this remains *the* approach to the Sunday service.

Although precipitated by somewhat different historical
circumstances and theological suppositions, Roman Catholic
worship also became individualistic and lacked the laity's
corporate involvement. The Sunday worship in the Mass
centered almost exclusively upon the priest at the altar. The
official liturgy of the Roman Church provided for congregational response and participation, but this was taken over by
altar servers or choirs. Since the priest celebrated the Mass
in Latin, by the sixteenth century and in modern times particularly, few laity understood the actions and prayers of the
service. The Latin language was not, however, the chief reason that the laity were excluded from participation in the
Mass. The chief reason was that by the post-Reformation
period, most Roman Catholic clergy believed that the people
should be spectators at the holy action which took place on
the altar.

It was in the role of spectators at Sunday worship that
Roman Catholics developed the strong individualism at worship so characteristic of Protestantism. The lay people did
not wish to remain mere onlookers at the Mass, and the
clergy agreed with them. The lay people were taught, therefore, to offer their own personal devotions during the service.
Through the use of prayer beads or personal prayer manuals,
the members of the congregation were to make their individual efforts at devotion while the priest celebrated Mass
at the altar. The context of Sunday worship was a liturgy
which had developed as the corporate worship of the Christian community, but which was being conducted almost
exclusively by an individual priest, while the congregation
carried on individual, personal devotions. All Roman Catholics involved in liturgical renewal have striven valiantly to

eliminate these incongruities in the corporate worship of the Roman Church.

The causes for the decline of corporate worship—individualism and lack of lay involvement—can be understood only in their historical context. Historical events and developments in the early, medieval, and Reformation Church gave rise to these factors. It is, then, a major purpose of the following chapters to illuminate the development of these causes in the history of Christian worship.

If the problems of liturgical renewal and the factors which caused the problems involve history, the solutions offered by the liturgical movement are even more historical in nature. In order to involve the laity in corporate worship and to overcome the individualism of public worship, the liturgical movement has looked to biblical and early church Christianity, where these problems did not exist. Many of the changes in forms, order, and content of services in Protestant and Anglican churches have taken place because of intensive study of the early period of Christianity, when there was a much stronger sense of visible Christian unity than today. For example, the recent enthusiastic emphasis in Anglicanism and somewhat in Protestantism upon the Eucharist, or Holy Communion, is a direct result of studies in early church worship. These studies clearly reveal that the Sunday service of every Christian congregation from biblical times to the Reformation was the Eucharist. Since Roman Catholic worship has retained much continuity with early Christian liturgy, the Roman Church has in one sense simply revived parts of her official liturgy (especially congregational ones) which had fallen into disuse or had lost significance. Recent Vatican Council and papal decrees have also eliminated some medieval accretions to the Roman Mass.

The revival or renewal of forms and patterns of worship

is only one phase of the liturgical movement. An even greater purpose has been to recapture the spirit and meaning of worship in biblical and early church Christianity. The forms and ceremonies of services, whether they are restorations or new creations, can be useless to the purpose of Christian worship unless they give meaning: unless corporate worship becomes the primary response of the individual, in and with the Christian community, to faith, and unless the basic offering of the Church is its corporate worship through Christ to the Father. The meaning or theology of worship has become, therefore, even more important to the liturgical movement than the visible signs of liturgical renewal.

Our chief aim, then, is to place Christian worship in its historical and theological perspective, because any understanding of liturgical renewal demands such a perspective. The problems, causes, and proposed solutions of the liturgical movement are rooted in history. Also, no matter how exciting liturgical renewal has been for modern Christianity, it has caused confusion, even division, within churches. The proponents of this renewal often point to biblical Christianity and the early Church as their criteria without sufficiently acquainting the Church with the liturgical history of those times. Simultaneously, medieval, Reformation, and post-Reformation liturgical developments, of which all Christians today are heirs, have been deprecated, again often without sufficient explanation.

Liturgical renewal is not merely a passing phase in modern Christianity; it will endure. Its acceptance will be more easily achieved, however, if Christian worship is understood in its historical perspective.

Chapter 1

New Testament Times

THE FIRST CHRISTIANS were Jews; Christianity came out of Judaism. Thus, it is not surprising to learn from the New Testament that the earliest Christians worshiped initially in the temple and in the synagogues of Jerusalem. Temple worship was strictly sacrificial. It involved sacramental ideas, symbolism, color, and ceremony, all of which influenced later Christian worship. Although the ordinary temple sacrifices consisted of offering grain or fruit, the liturgy of animal sacrifice was the most dramatic and colorful. It involved the three symbolic acts of offering, destruction, and acquiring new life. In offering the animal the Jew transferred himself symbolically to the animal, thereby freeing himself of impurity and sin. The animal was then killed, an act in which the offerer died symbolically and his impurity or sin was done away. Finally the offerer feasted on the meat of the slaughtered animal, an act which symbolically effected his communion with God.

9

This highly sacramental and sacrificial temple worship strongly influenced early Christian theology and worship. The writer of the Epistle to the Hebrews, for instance, interpreted temple worship in terms of Christ: by his death and resurrection Christ made the one, true offering and sacrifice for all men through which mankind was reconciled, made one, with God. Thus, the writer of Hebrews asserted that the temple sacrifices were no longer necessary, for they had lost their meaning and efficacy.

St. Paul interpreted Christian worship in terms of Christ's sacrifice but against the background of temple sacrificial worship. In his letter to the Romans (Chapter 6), Paul states that in Baptism the Christian symbolically dies and rises with Christ; the Christian participates in the sacrifice of Christ by means of the words and actions of the baptismal service. Paul also related the Eucharist, or Lord's Supper, to Christ's sacrifice, for in his first letter to the Corinthians (Chapter 11), he says that in the Eucharist Christians "proclaim the Lord's death until he comes."

Temple worship influenced Christian worship not only in matters of sacrifice and sacrament but also in terms of color and ceremony. The Jews loved extensive ceremonial details and vivid color in their worship, and these characteristics were carried over into Christian worship by the first Christians. The hymns which the Jews sang in their worship were what we call the Psalms, for the Psalter was the hymnal of temple worship. Thus, the Psalms, which so greatly enrich Christian worship, are also a legacy of the Jewish temple.

The Jews sang Psalms not only in the temple but also in their synagogue worship. In fact, the worship of the synagogue influenced to a large extent the formation of many aspects of early Christian worship. The reading of Scripture (Jewish Scripture consisted only of the Old Testament books) and the interpretation or explanation of Scripture (what we call a sermon) formed the two basic parts of synagogue worship. The fact that the reading and preaching of Scripture is so important in Christian worship stems directly from the Jewish practice.

When the Jews prayed in their synagogues, or even in the temple, they stood for prayer, probably with their arms outstretched. Therefore, standing for prayer was naturally adopted by the early Christians. It was not for several hundred years, as we shall see, and it was due to other influences, that Christians began to kneel for prayer. The Jews, moreover, did not just say prayers or read Scripture; they sang or chanted them. Christianity adopted this practice also, and throughout most of the first thousand years of Christian worship, the prayers and lessons from Scripture were sung or chanted. The "said service" actually began in the Middle Ages. It is certainly a curious fact of history that what we today find commonplace—the said service—was unknown in the early Church; yet what we often believe to be highly elaborate and special—the sung service—was the norm in the Church for hundreds of years.

At the end of their chanted prayers, the synagogue congregation made its assent by singing out "Amen," which roughly translated from the Hebrew means "So be it." Throughout history, Christians have borrowed the Hebrew "Amen" as their expression of assent in public worship.

Like temple and synagogue worship, Jewish home worship also influenced the development of Christian corporate worship. Ordinarily the Jewish family prayed at home three times a day, and fasted twice a week, on Mondays and Thursdays. All meals in a Jewish home had a religious significance. The Jews believed that all good things, like food, ultimately came from God. The home meal had a blessing of the food and often other prayers, as well as religious conversation.

Often at the main meal in a Jewish home, but always at

a formal meal, the host would pronounce a blessing over a loaf of bread, and then he would break it up and give pieces to the others present. At the end of the meal, the host would take a special cup of wine mixed with water (in the ancient world, people drank wine this way), and after pronouncing a blessing over it, he would pass the cup around the table for all to drink. Obviously we see here something of the setting of the Last Supper; yet the Last Supper was the basis for the beginning of a distinctive Christian worship. Thus, we turn to that Supper which is the foundation of our worship today.

The Last Supper

Although the earliest Christians at first continued to worship in temple and synagogue, almost immediately after Christ's death and resurrection they also began to develop a distinctive Christian worship in the form of a meal. In the Acts of the Apostles the term "breaking of bread" is used four times to refer to the Lord's Supper, or Holy Eucharist. We can best understand why the early Christians developed this distinctive worship in the form of a meal by looking carefully at the New Testament accounts of the Last Supper.

The two most significant aspects of the Last Supper are its setting and what Jesus did and said at the meal. The Supper took place at the time of the Jewish Passover on a Thursday evening (Maundy Thursday), the night before Jesus' crucifixion (Good Friday). The Passover setting aided Jesus in his interpretation of the Supper to the disciples, and this setting also influenced the early Christians to understand their worship of God in the light of the Lord's Supper. The main theme of Passover was redemption. Each year at Passover the Jews celebrated their past redemption, the time when their forefathers, led by Moses, were delivered by God from the Egyptians. The Jews, however, did not just look back to the past in their Passover celebration, for another major theme was their looking forward to the full and final salvation of the Jews at the last great day. These two Passover themes of past redemption and future salvation became very important in the Christian understanding of the Last Supper and the Holy Eucharist.

More important than the setting, though, were Jesus' actions and words at this meal. There are four accounts in the New Testament of what the Lord did and said: in the first three Gospels of Matthew, Mark, and Luke, and in Paul's first letter to the Corinthians. The Gospel of John mentions the fact of the meal but does not describe it. The writer of the Fourth Gospel emphasizes what happened after the meal: Jesus' washing the disciples' feet and his discourses. Why this Gospel does not give an account of the Lord's actions at the meal has long been in dispute among scholars. Perhaps by the time the Fourth Gospel was written, the Eucharist had become so important in the Church that only baptized Christians were permitted to know about it. We do know that by the third century the Church kept her liturgical rites secret from all except the baptized, but we do not know whether this idea was prevalent in the first century. On the other hand, it may be that since the other Gospels described the meal so clearly, the fourth evangelist chose to emphasize the foot-washing and the discourses because these were not mentioned in the earlier Gospels.

The four accounts offer a somewhat clear picture of Jesus' actions at the Supper. At a solemn point during the meal, he took a loaf of bread, he gave thanks for it, he broke the bread into pieces, and he gave the pieces to the disciples. Then as the meal ended, he took a cup of wine (which would have been mixed with water according to custom), he gave thanks for it, and he passed it among the disciples.

As he performed these actions, Jesus also interpreted them to the disciples in a few poignant sentences. As he took, blessed, broke, and gave the bread, he said, "This is my body." As he took, blessed, and gave the cup, he said, "This is my blood of the new covenant, which is poured out for many."

In these actions and words, Jesus was acting out prophetically the meaning of his own impending sacrifice, his crucifixion and resurrection. Because of his confrontation of the Jewish leaders, Jesus knew that his end was near. Thus, he took the opportunity of the Supper in its Passover setting to use bread and wine and words as the means to relate what was about to happen to him. He used these dramatic symbols to portray his own passion, death, and resurrection.

According to Paul's account of the Last Supper in 1 Corinthians, Jesus also said, as he distributed the bread and wine, "Do this in remembrance of me" (1 Cor. 11:24-25). In other words, according to Paul, Jesus commanded his disciples to repeat the Supper continually and thus to make it central in their lives. Some scholars believe that Jesus did not command "Do this," because these words do not appear in the accounts of the Last Supper in Matthew and Mark nor in the early versions of Luke. Although this issue can never be fully resolved, one important fact should be recognized. Jesus' death and resurrection took place around the year 30, and just a little over twenty years later, Paul was writing 1 Corinthians, in which he declared (11:23) that he had received his account of the Last Supper from the Church's tradition. Thus, the dominical command "Do this" was part of the Church's most primitive tradition. The earliest Christians believed the Lord had said that his Supper must be repeated continuously.

Perhaps of greater importance in the command "Do this in remembrance of me" is its word "remembrance." In

English this is a rather weak word which means a vague looking back to past events. But as Paul used the word "remembrance," it was much stronger and more meaningful. The Greek word for remembrance is *anamnesis,* and it means an objective recalling or re-presentation. For Paul, at the Lord's Supper, the Church objectively recalls and re-presents Jesus' Last Supper. But at the Last Supper, Jesus used the dramatic symbols of bread, wine, and words to portray his own sacrifice. Therefore, as the Church re-enacts the Last Supper in the Eucharist, she also recalls and re-presents symbolically the Lord's death and resurrection. In his account of the Supper, Paul actually declared, "For as often as you eat this bread and drink the cup, you proclaim the Lord's death until he comes." The Church's worship is a means of re-presenting and proclaiming Christ's sacrificial death and resurrection.

We see then that the Passover theme of redemption was reflected in the early Christians' understanding of their worship in the Lord's Supper. Unlike the Jews, who recalled their deliverance from Egypt, the Christians, in the Eucharist, objectively remembered the Lord's acts of crucifixion and resurrection done once for all men. To the Christian, Christ's death and resurrection were redemptive acts, for by them man was freed from the bondage of sin and corruption, and he was freed for the possibility of becoming a new person in Christ. Thus, in the Church's worship the means of redemption were recalled and symbolically re-presented.

The New Testament accounts of the Last Supper also refer to the Passover theme of future salvation. Paul says that in the eucharistic act the Church proclaims the Lord's death "until he comes." The Eucharist looked forward, therefore, to the Lord's second coming and man's final salvation, which meant eternal life with God. Paul's idea probably came from Jesus' own explanatory words at the Last Supper.

The first three Gospels all record that at the meal Jesus said
to his disciples, "I say to you, I shall not drink again of the
fruit of the vine until that day when I drink it new in the
kingdom of God" (Mark 14:25). In other words, Jesus also
looked upon the Last Supper as a foretaste of the Messianic
Banquet. Many of the Jews of Jesus' day (and Jesus was a
Jew) believed that at the end of the world the Jews who
would be saved would have a great banquet with their
messiah. Jesus indicated that the Last Supper was a sign or
foretaste of that banquet.

Thus, as Jesus interpreted the Last Supper and as the early
Christians understood it, the two main Passover themes of
redemption and future salvation predominate. Furthermore,
since in the Eucharist the Church re-enacts the Last Supper,
the Eucharist itself involves both redemption through the
recalling of the Lord's sacrifice and final salvation in that it
is a foretaste of the Messianic Banquet.

Many of the eucharistic references in the New Testament
indicate that the earliest Christians strongly believed that
the Lord was really present in their worship. This is evident,
for example, in the references to the Lord's resurrection ap-
pearances in Luke 24:35, Mark 16:14, Acts 10:41, as well as
in the symbolic eucharistic reference in the Book of Revelation (3:20). Christ was present for the early Church either
because of *anamnesis,* an objective and symbolic recalling
and re-presentation of his death and resurrection, or because the Eucharist was a foretaste of the Messianic Banquet,
and the Messiah had to be present at his banquet. Therefore,
in the New Testament there are strong indications that
when the early Christians worshiped in the Lord's Supper,
they believed they were feasting with Christ. Their risen
Lord and Saviour was their host at the sacred meal.

In the Gospel of John this theme changed from feasting
with Christ in the Eucharist to feasting on Christ. The well-

known eucharistic discourse in the sixth chapter of the Fourth Gospel emphasizes that it is Christ who is received at the banquet. "I am the living bread which came down from heaven; if any one eats of this bread, he will live forever; and the bread which I shall give for the life of the world is my flesh" (6:51). "Truly, truly, I say to you, unless you eat the flesh of the Son of man and drink his blood, you have no life in you; he who eats my flesh and drinks my blood has eternal life, and I will raise him up at the last day. For my flesh is food indeed, and my blood is drink indeed. He who eats my flesh and drinks my blood abides in me, and I in him" (6:53-56). These references indicate that in the Gospel of John, Christ's presence at the Church's eucharistic meal is not just as host; he is also the feast.

This approach to the Eucharist as set forth in the Fourth Gospel is crucial for understanding the development of Christian worship. The Gospel of John's emphasis upon the actual food of the eucharistic meal and the strong identification of Christ with the bread and wine soon became the early Church's major understanding of her eucharistic worship. The other approach, which emphasized the whole banquet with Christ present as host, did not long remain as an important understanding of the Church's worship. Thus, even in New Testament times the Church came to emphasize the bread and wine in her worship rather than the whole service.

It is significant, however, that whether the New Testament Church believed Christ to be the host or the food of the Lord's Supper, all agreed he was truly present. In the later ages of the Church's history and until our own day, sharp and divisive disagreement has been carried on by various Christians and various churches about the presence of Christ in the Eucharist. The early Christians had no such disagreement. They believed their Lord was present, but they did not go into detailed descriptions of how he was present. This problem, as we shall see, developed in later ages, when Christians attempted to set forth precise and dogmatic definitions concerning the Lord's presence at their worship.

THE SERVICE IN NEW TESTAMENT TIMES

Although the earliest Christians first worshiped in temple and synagogue as well as in their own service of the Lord's Supper, not many decades passed before the Eucharist was their only manner of corporate worship. Long before the temple was destroyed A.D. 70, Christianity had spread far beyond Jerusalem. Moreover, although Christian preachers went to the Jewish synagogues of the Roman world in order to gain converts, they were soon put out of these synagogues because the Jews believed them to be subverters of the Hebrew religion. The Church's worship therefore became exclusively its own distinctive eucharistic service.

It would be of great help to our understanding of early Christian worship if we knew precisely what were the order and the content of the service in the first-century Church. Unfortunately the New Testament writers do not tell us very much about these matters. Although it is possible that the writers may have wanted to keep the details of the service a secret from all but the baptized, it is more likely that since the order and content of the service were not controversial matters, there was no need to write about them. Corporate worship was a normal thing in which all Christians engaged; there was no need to describe its details. Paul wrote so much about the meaning of the Lord's Supper in 1 Corinthians only because of a behavior problem in the Corinthian congregation at the time the eucharistic meal was celebrated (11:17-22). The more affluent members of the congregation were using the meal as an occasion for a party, to the neglect of the poorer members and in opposition to the real meaning of the eucharistic meal.

From these fragmentary references in the New Testament as well as from later sources, we can determine something of the nature of the service in the first century. Christians worshiped together in the context of a meal, but it was a very special meal which at an early time developed definite forms and characteristics. This eucharistic meal probably took place on Sunday, the first day of the week, the day of the Resurrection. The meal would have been preceded by the reading of Scripture and preaching; no doubt the singing of Psalms and hymns took place before and after the meal.

The most important part of the meal was the prayer of blessing over the bread and the cup. During this prayer the actions and words of Christ at the Last Supper were recited, and at the end of the prayer the congregation sang out its "Amen."

The setting for this eucharistic meal was a house. Since the early Christians were few and their religion was not legally recognized by the Roman government, the Church could have no buildings of her own. At first the early Christians would have worshiped in the house of any of their members. Later, no doubt, a large house of one of the members was needed for the growing Church. Probably by the second century in some cities, Christian worship was carried on in a house designated strictly for the purpose of worship. Yet until the late second century, most congregations worshiped in an ordinary house, which when not being used for worship was the regular place of living for the owner. Today we know of no distinctive church buildings before the third century and of no building of churches on a large scale until the Church was legally recognized in the fourth century. Thus, the house-church was the setting for Christian worship for over two hundred years in many places and for over three hundred years in other places.

The atmosphere of the service in the New Testament Church was one of joy and thanksgiving. By the second century the service was called the Eucharist, a word derived from the Greek *eucharistia,* which means "thanksgiving." This was a service of thanksgiving because Christians knew that their risen Lord was present. They were feasting with him; they were feasting on him. In this early period of Christian worship, there was very little emphasis on sin, confession, and repentance, which in later centuries came to surround the services of the Church. Nor was there that inhibiting sense of awe which so much characterized the later eucharistic services. The early Christians were happy to come together for the eucharistic meal because they were re-enacting the Last Supper and participating symbolically in the Lord's death and resurrection—the acts which had brought their own redemption.

Chapter 2

The Second Century:
Sacrament and Service

DISTINCTIVE Christian worship first developed in the context of a community meal or supper. Before the end of the first century, however, the growing Church realized that her corporate worship could not continue strictly as a community meal. It was necessary for the sacramental service (the Holy Communion or Eucharist proper) to be separated from the fellowship meal.

A number of factors brought about this separation. Long before the end of the first century, most Christians were gentile converts. Although the first Christians were Jews and the earliest Christian preaching was done among the Jews, it became evident by A.D. 50 that the gentiles of the Roman Empire were much more responsive to the Gospel of Christ. The gentiles had been converted from various pagan religions in which no tradition existed for the kind of religious family

21

meal that was prevalent in Judaism, and from which the
Christian Eucharist had developed. Worship in the context
of a regular meal was more suited to Jewish Christianity than
to gentile Christianity. St. Paul's description of the abuses
surrounding the eucharistic meal in the gentile congregation
at Corinth probably typified a widespread problem in the
Church. Pagan meals, especially festival ones, were rather
raucous and not conducive to the kind of worship called for
by the Lord's Supper.

A practical problem also arose before the end of the first
century. The Church grew in goodly numbers in some large
cities and towns such as Antioch, Corinth, Ephesus, Rome,
and probably Alexandria. This growth prevented all the
Christians in a congregation from having a regular meal
together at which each person had a place at a table in the
house-church. The Church was facing the familiar problem
of not having enough space. Moreover, since the early Church
stressed the unity of the Christian community in a city, vil-
lage, or town, the thought of splitting into smaller congregations or parish churches did not appeal to them. Not until the
third century, and in some places not until the fourth century, did the Church establish more than one congregation in
a town or city. Thus, gentile-oriented Christianity and the
problem of space chiefly led to the establishment of a sacramental service which was separated from the fellowship
meal.

We should keep in mind, however, that the Church's worship in the Eucharist has always remained within the context
of a meal. We continue to re-enact the Last Supper at each
Eucharist. The altar is the table around which the congregation gathers. On the altar is food—bread and wine—which
is taken, blessed, and eaten by all. No essential change was
made in the shift from a meal to a sacramental service.
Instead of having a complete meal in a house-church, with
enough tables for each person to have a place, the sacra-

mental service involved one small table around which all gathered for a small but highly meaningful meal of bread and wine.

As with most changes or developments in the early Church, this separation took place but gradually in the various Christian communities of the Roman world. We do not have the records to know when or where the separation began. There are some references in the New Testament that imply a change to a sacramental service, but it is not until the early second century that most sources clearly reveal a separation of the sacramental service from the fellowship meal. We would be safe in saying that this change developed throughout the Church from A.D. 50 to 110.

EUCHARISTIC THEMES

Most of the Christian writers of the second century dealt with Christian worship, especially the Eucharist, in the same way as did the New Testament writers; that is, they were chiefly concerned with the meaning or theology of worship. Hence, they wrote little about the order and content of the service. The study of the eucharistic themes taught by these writers is quite fascinating.

The second-century Church's understanding of Eucharist and worship was directly related to the New Testament Church and developed out of it. For example, the chief Christian writers of the second century—Clement of Rome, Ignatius of Antioch, Justin Martyr, Irenaeus, as well as the anonymous author of a writing called *The Teaching of the Twelve Apostles* or *The Didache*—all declare the centrality of the Eucharist not only in Christian worship but in the over-all life of Christians and the Church. As in New Testament times the atmosphere of the service continued to be one of joy and thanksgiving.

Throughout Christian history, from New Testament times until our own day, three theological themes have dominated the Church's understanding of eucharistic worship. They are the presence of Christ at the service and in the sacrament of bread and wine, the Eucharist as a sacrificial service or rite, and the benefits received by the Christian from the Holy Communion. Although these themes were stated explicitly or implicitly in the New Testament, they were greatly developed by the second-century Church.

Christ was present in the Eucharist for the New Testament Church either as the host at the banquet—the Church feasted with her Lord—or, as in the Gospel of John, he was identified with the bread and wine—the Church feasted on Christ. The second-century Church strongly followed the Johannine view in believing Christ to be present in the bread and wine. Ignatius, the Bishop of Antioch at the beginning of the century, wrote, "What I want is God's bread, which is the flesh of Christ . . . and for drink I want his blood. . . ." (Letter to the Romans 7:3). At mid-century, Justin, an outstanding Christian layman, teacher, and later a martyr, wrote, ". . . we do not receive these things as common bread or common drink; but as Jesus Christ our Saviour being incarnate by God's word took flesh and blood for our salvation, so also we have been taught that the food consecrated by the word of prayer which comes from him, from which our flesh and blood are nourished by transformation, is the flesh and blood of that incarnate Jesus" (I Apology 66). Justin's use of the word "transformation" is not related to the later medieval doctrine of Transubstantiation, which stated that the essence of bread and wine were changed into the very essence of the Body and Blood of Christ; however, Justin strongly proclaims that Christ is in some way present in the bread and wine.

As stated above, the idea of the Eucharist as a sacrifice was implied in the New Testament. The first-century Church believed that through *anamnesis,* objective remembrance, the sacrifice of Christ was symbolically re-presented in the

Eucharist. The New Testament writers, however, did not call the Eucharist a sacrifice, but the second-century writers frequently did. In the very short fourteenth chapter of the *Didache*, the Eucharist is called a sacrifice four times. Justin wrote that Christians "in every place offer sacrifices to him, i.e., the bread of the Eucharist, and also the cup of the Eucharist" (Dialogue 41).

The second-century writers did not precisely define what they meant by the Eucharist as a sacrifice, although, as throughout Christian history, they usually related sacrifice to an offering. It was not until the medieval period that the Church was led to define rigidly and dogmatically the eucharistic sacrifice. The second-century writers unanimously agreed that the eucharistic sacrifice was a spiritual one in contrast to the physical, animal sacrifices of the Jews and pagans. Some writers gave reasons for calling the Eucharist a sacrifice. Justin, for example, related it to Jesus' sacrifice in that at the Eucharist the Church, through *anamnesis*, recalls the Lord's death and resurrection. Yet in another place Justin, like the Book of Common Prayer, referred to the Eucharist as an offering of praise and thanksgiving. Irenaeus and Ignatius also used both of these themes to explain the eucharistic sacrifice. Irenaeus, however, added a third idea. He regarded the Eucharist as the Christian offering of the first fruits of God's creation, for the bread and wine came from the grain and vines of the soil of creation.

The second-century writers proclaimed, then, the eucharistic sacrifice in the offering of prayer, praise, thanksgiving, and the first fruits of creation. It was a sacrifice because Christ's sacrifice was objectively recalled in the doing of the eucharistic service. The refreshing thing about these writers is that they did not seek to impose a single idea of eucharistic sacrifice as the only acceptable and true one. They reflected many theories and many themes. The Church's troubles over eucharistic doctrine arose later when she began to establish one theory as the only correct doctrine to the exclusion of others.

The fruits of Communion, the belief that there is benefit for the partaker of the food of the Lord's Supper, were emphasized by the New Testament writers. In Matthew's Gospel, "the forgiveness of sins" is considered a benefit of Communion (26:28). For the Fourth Gospel, eternal life is the fruit of the Supper—"He who eats my flesh and drinks my blood has eternal life" (6:54). St. Paul expressed another viewpoint when he described the Eucharist as both a means and an expression of the unity of the Church (1 Cor. 10:17).

The second-century Church continued this New Testament emphasis on the fruits of the eucharistic feast. That the Church's worship is a means and expression of Christian unity was urged both by Ignatius of Antioch (Letter to the Ephesians 5, 13, 20) and in the *Didache* (Chapter 9). With dramatic phrases, Ignatius also emphasized eternal life as a benefit of Communion when he referred to it as "the medicine of immortality" (Letter to the Ephesians 20) and "an immortal love feast indeed" (Letter to the Romans 7). The *Didache* presents the same theme in a prayer which thanks God for having "given spiritual food and drink and eternal life through Jesus" (Chapter 10). Irenaeus claimed that "our bodies, when they receive the Eucharist, are no longer corruptible, having the hope of the resurrection to eternity" (Against the Heresies 4:18:5).

Justin and Irenaeus introduced the idea of a somewhat new and different benefit of Communion which involved the strengthening of our present earthly existence through the reception of Communion. Justin declared that "our flesh and blood are nourished" by the Communion (I Apology 66), while Irenaeus claimed that "the substance of our flesh is increased and supported" by the eucharistic feast (Against the Heresies 5:2:3).

The foregoing testifies to the Church's keen interest in the meaning of her worship during the second century. Whether they spoke of the presence of Christ, the eucharistic sacrifice, or the benefit of Communion, churchmen were deeply concerned about this central act of the Christian life.

THE ORDER OF SERVICE

Only one writer, Justin, wrote about the actual order of service in the second-century Church. The *Didache*, an earlier document, contains what seem to be some early eucharistic prayers, but it does not contain a clear order of service. Justin, however, in his *First Apology*, a defense of Christianity addressed to the Roman emperor, presents in careful detail the eucharistic service as celebrated in the city of Rome at the time he was writing, about A.D. 150.

Justin wrote about two types of Eucharist, the Easter service and the regular Sunday service. As do the other documents of the time, the *First Apology* tells us that when Christians gathered for worship they offered the Eucharist. The normal day for Christian worship was Sunday because it was the first day of the week—the day when God began creation and the day "our Saviour rose from the dead" (I Apology 67).

On an ordinary Sunday the service began with reading from Scripture. Justin says that the prophetic writings of the Old Testament and the "memoirs of the apostles," by which he probably meant selections from either the Gospels, the Book of Acts, or letters of Paul, were read. After the lessons the president of the service (the bishop in the second-century Church) would deliver a sermon on the meaning of the lessons which had been read. We may note that this lesson-sermon beginning to the service obviously came from synagogue worship. Justin also informs us that when a baptism preceded the Eucharist, as on Easter, there was no

Scripture reading or sermon. In other words, the beginning of the service was not, as in some services today, rigidly set with a fixed pattern.

When the Easter Baptism or Sunday sermon was ended, the service continued with intercessory prayers. Although Justin does not tell us the exact nature and content of these prayers, later documents indicate that the deacon would chant biddings to pray for various categories of people such as the newly baptized, the clergy, the congregation, the sick, and the rulers. After each bidding, there would be silence while the members of the congregation offered their own private intercessions. Then the president (the bishop) would audibly summarize these intercessions with a short, terse prayer. In other words, he would collect the individual silent prayers into an audible summary prayer. Later, this prayer would be called a collect. It is significant that intercessory prayer was part of the earliest recorded eucharistic service. In fact this type of prayer has been found in most eucharistic services ever since.

These prayers were followed by the kiss of peace, a symbolic act found in all the early eucharistic liturgies, but which remains in only a few modern services. The kiss of peace was an ancient way of greeting, something like our shaking hands. The kiss was actually something of a gentle hug, similar to the form of greeting still observed in some European countries. At the Christian Eucharist the kiss of peace, begun by the bishop and passed by him to the clergy and from them to the congregation, symbolized the fellowship and unity of the Christian community.

In the early Church the intercessory prayer and kiss of peace as well as regular Sunday Scripture lessons and sermon were all preparatory or preliminary to the main part of the service called the Eucharist proper, which began with the offertory. In the service of the Holy Communion today, the Communion proper also begins with the offertory. All that goes before, through creed and/or sermon, is known as the Ante-Communion (*ante* is a Latin word meaning "before").

Throughout Christian history the basic purpose of the offertory has been to gather and to place the bread and wine on the altar. When the Eucharist was strictly a fellowship meal, the people brought their own food to the Supper. This idea carried over into the sacramental service of the second century and later. The members of the congregation brought their own loaves of bread and small flagons of mixed wine and water. These eucharistic provisions were collected by the deacons, probably when the people entered the door of the house-church. At the offertory the deacons brought enough bread and wine to the president for that service. What remained of the people's offering was given to the poor or to the clergy, who were still unsalaried in the second century. The small loaves baked by the women of the congregation were leavened bread; it was not until the Middle Ages that the Western Church began to use unleavened bread at the Eucharist.

After the brief act of offertory, the bishop offered the Eucharistic Prayer (or as it is called today, the Prayer of Consecration), during which the Lord's acts and words at the Last Supper were recited. Justin does not give the actual content of this prayer. (Shortly we shall note a text of this prayer from the early third century.) Justin does say, however, that the president offered the prayer "to the best of his ability," which means that the prayer was extemporaneous. In the early Church until the end of the fourth century, the prayers of corporate worship were not universally fixed. They were composed by each local bishop and may or may not have been put into written form. The Eucharistic Prayer ended with the congregation's singing out "Amen." Since Justin was a layman he made a great point of the "Amen" as the congregation's essential participation in the prayer.

The Eucharistic Prayer in the early Church was called

the prayer, not only because it was always the most solemn and important prayer of the service but also because in Justin's time it was the only prayer in the main part of the service. Immediately following the Eucharistic Prayer, the people received the Holy Communion, which was distributed by the deacons. The manner of receiving Communion is not mentioned by Justin, but, as in later times, the people probably came and stood around the Holy Table. Apparently some bread and wine always remained after everyone had communicated, for Justin states that after both the Easter and ordinary Sunday Eucharists, the deacons carried what was left "to the absent." The absent no doubt were the sick or infirm. We see here an early idea of Sick Communion in the Church. The faithful Christians who could not be present were still a part of the community's Eucharist. Therefore, the sacrament was brought to them after the service.

The Communion ended the service. The people went out immediately into the world to their work or to their homes. There were no prayers or blessing or ceremonies after the Communion. These things were foreign to the primitive Church. The Eucharist emphasized action, not words. Everything culminated in action; therefore, the Communion was the climax and end of the service.

Justin tells us that at the regular Sunday service, as the people left the house-church, "those who prosper, and who so wish, contribute, each one as much as he chooses to." The money collected was used to care for orphans and widows in the Christian community. This interesting early custom is significant for two reasons. First, the collection of money took place after the service; the bread and wine, not money, were the offertory in the service. Second, the people's contribution was another action symbolizing the worshiping community's going out into the world from the communion table, for the money which was collected formed part of a Christian social-service program.

Justin's description of the Eucharist is exceedingly significant. We see that by the mid-second century the Church had
a definite order of service. Moreover, it was a service which
had been long established. Justin was not creating anything;
he was recording tradition. The same form of service no
doubt prevailed throughout the Christian Church in the
Roman world at that time. Justin had been born in the East
and was converted to Christianity in Asia Minor. He had
traveled as a Christian from Ephesus to Rome; therefore, if
the service had been different in other places, he would have
noted it in his Apology to the emperor. Furthermore, we
know from another source that in the year 154 Polycarp, the
Bishop of Smyrna in Asia Minor, traveled to Rome to discuss
the dating of Easter with Anicetus, the Bishop of Rome. Although the two bishops could not find common agreement
on the matter, Anicetus nevertheless had Polycarp celebrate
the Eucharist in the church of Rome. The Roman bishop
would probably not have allowed Polycarp to preside at the
service if the Eastern service had been different from that of
Rome.

We ought to note the brevity of the service in Justin's day.
On an ordinary Sunday it began with Scripture lessons and
a sermon followed by the intercessory prayer. Then came
two brief but highly significant actions, the kiss of peace and
the offertory. These were followed by the Eucharistic Prayer,
the people's "Amen," and the Communion. It was brief, but
all the essential parts of eucharistic worship were present.
The later ages of the Church's life would add much to the
service, but all its services up to our day contain the brief
and essential pattern of the second century.

The Third Century:
The Apostolic Tradition

The Apostolic Tradition, a work written about 215 by Hippolytus, a presbyter of the Church in Rome, has won the praise of modern scholars as the most important document for the history of early Christian worship. Hippolytus not only wrote about the outline of the service, as did Justin, but also gave the text or content of the prayers. *The Apostolic Tradition* describes not only the Eucharist but also the services of Baptism, Confirmation, and the ordination of a bishop, presbyter, or deacon. The document tells us about some church rules, especially on fasting, and about the daily devotions of the laity. It is not surprising that Hippolytus' *Apostolic Tradition* has been called a kind of Book of Common Prayer for the early Church.

In this writing, Hippolytus sought to show what the services of the Church had been for a long time. The services of
his day, he said, were in the tradition of the apostles, the
first-century Church. He did not say that they were identical
to the first-century services, but that they were in the same
tradition. Since in his other writings Hippolytus shows that
he was a very conservative person, and since he lived between about 155 and 235, we can be sure that he is describ-
ing how Christians in the city of Rome worshiped throughout the latter half of the second century and well into the
third. This fact is well illustrated by the great similarity in
order of service between Justin's account and that of *The
Apostolic Tradition.*

Hippolytus also described two types of eucharistic service, but unlike Justin he did not give an account of an ordinary Sunday service. Hippolytus' descriptions are of an
ordination Eucharist and the Easter service. Thus, one service begins with the consecration of a bishop and the other
with Baptism and Confirmation, but there is no mention of
Scripture lessons and a sermon, which, according to Justin,
were the ordinary beginning of the Sunday service.

We know from other third-century sources, however, that
the preliminary, or Ante-Communion, part of the regular
Sunday service was basically the reading of lessons, a sermon,
and finally the intercessory prayers. This preparatory part
had become by the third century an important part of
church life and was called the Service of the Catechumens.
Catechumens were adult converts from paganism or Judaism
to Christianity who were being instructed prior to their Baptism and Confirmation. The period of instruction and preparation for Baptism ordinarily lasted a year, but *The Apostolic Tradition* calls for a catechumenate of three years.
Catechumens attended Sunday worship with the regular

faithful Christians, but the catechumens had to leave the
service after the lessons, sermon, and intercessions. The Eucharist proper, beginning with the actions of kiss of peace
and offertory, was called the Service of the Faithful, for only
baptized Christians were permitted to worship at the main
part of the service.

The service in *The Apostolic Tradition* is generally the
same as that described by Justin. After the preliminary ordination or Baptism and Confirmation come the intercessory
prayers, which are followed by the symbolic kiss of peace
and the offertory. Then follows the Eucharistic Prayer with
the people's "Amen." Hippolytus gives us a text for this
prayer, which we shall discuss presently. Following the
Eucharistic Prayer is one action not mentioned in Justin's
account: the celebrant (the bishop) breaks the bread. Immediately after this fraction (the technical term for the
breaking of the bread at the Eucharist), the service comes
to its climax and ends with the administration of Communion. Although Hippolytus does not give rubrics or directions for the reception of the sacrament, other contemporary
sources reveal that the Communion was received standing
and the communion bread was received in the right hand.

Hippolytus and Justin reveal the brevity of the Church's
worship in their centuries. There were excellent reasons for
a short service. First, the early Church emphasized action,
not words, in her worship. This eucharistic action was what
Christ did at the Last Supper. Even the order of service
followed the Lord's actions. As Jesus had *taken* bread and
wine, so the Church began the Eucharist proper with the
offertory, the placing of the bread and wine on the altar. As
Jesus had *blessed* the bread and wine, so the Church developed the *Eucharistic Prayer*. As Jesus had *broken* the
bread, so by Hippolytus' time the celebrant was *breaking*
the bread after the prayer. Finally, as Jesus *gave* the bread

and wine to the disciples, the Church ended the service with the administration of the *Holy Communion.* In the early Church everyone, clergy and laity, acted and participated in the brief service. Their service was a far cry from much of our modern worship, in which the minister (be he bishop, priest, or deacon) reads, says, or preaches the service while the congregation just listens as spectators.

An additional reason for the brevity of the service was that before the fourth century, Christianity was not a legal religion in the Roman Empire, and the Church endured actual persecution from time to time. In fact she always lived under the threat of persecution. In these circumstances a brief service of action, which reached its climax in the Communion, followed by a quick departure for home or work, was necessary. We shall find that when the Church won legal status in the fourth century, her services become longer.

Although Hippolytus states that the Eucharistic Prayer was still offered extemporaneously by the bishop, in *The Apostolic Tradition* he nevertheless gives us a model text of such a prayer. This model text is significant because it reveals the main themes present in the central prayer of the service, no matter how the prayer was actually worded by the bishop. The most startling revelation in the prayer is that its six themes are still the main themes of the Prayer of Consecration in the service of the Holy Communion in the Book of Common Prayer. In fact, almost all eucharistic liturgies throughout Christian history contain the very same six themes. This is highly significant, for it shows that at a very early time the Church established the main themes for the principal prayer of the service.

The prayer begins with a preliminary dialogue between the bishop and congregation.

Bishop: The Lord be with you.
Congregation: And with thy spirit.

Bishop: Lift up your hearts.
Congregation: We lift them up unto the Lord.
Bishop: Let us give thanks to the Lord.
Congregation: It is meet and right.

This introductory dialogue is known as the Sursum Corda (Lift up your hearts). It is present in every known liturgical text, and was no doubt the first fixed wording in the Christian Eucharist.

After this dialogue the prayer proper develops the idea of thanksgiving; it is the Eucharistic Prayer and "eucharist" means thanksgiving. Hippolytus' text gives thanks for Christ the Redeemer of mankind and mentions his birth, death, and resurrection. The Prayer of Consecration in the Prayer Book begins with the same thanksgiving for redemption, but emphasizes only the death of Christ. The next theme for both Hippolytus' and the Prayer Book's service is the recital of Jesus' actions and words at the Last Supper.

The next two themes of *anamnesis* (stating that the Eucharist is an objective recalling or remembrance of Christ's death and resurrection) and offering of the bread and the cup also follow in the Prayer Book, but in reverse order. The "holy gifts" are first offered, and then remembrance is made of the Lord's death, resurrection, and ascension.

Hippolytus' text continues with a petition that God will send his Holy Spirit to bless both the Church's offering—the bread and wine—and the people, that they may faithfully receive the sacramental food. Although the Prayer Book wording differs, it does have an invocation of the Holy Spirit at this point in the prayer. Such an invocation of the Holy Spirit is called an *epiclesis* in a liturgical service. Both prayers end with a final glorious doxology, praising God through Christ and in the Spirit who dwells in the Church.

This model of a eucharistic prayer given by Hippolytus

illustrates again the meaning of eucharistic worship in the early Church. For example, the recital of the Lord's actions and words at the Last Supper and the objective remembrance of his death and resurrection in the *anamnesis* signified Christ's presence. The offering of the bread and the cup emphasized the sacrificial aspect of the Eucharist. The people's sacrifice was symbolized by their offering of bread and wine for the service, and the bread and cup also symbolized Christ's sacrifice of death and resurrection.

The Apostolic Tradition offers us a clear picture of the Church's worship in the second and third centuries. The outline or order of service and the theological themes in these centuries had been established in a brief service of action. It is significant that in the last ten years, at a few ecumenical gatherings where Christians of all persuasions were present, the service according to Hippolytus was used as an experiment in ecumenical eucharistic worship. This is readily understandable, for the Hippolytan rite represents the service of the whole Church before the Church was divided into many denominations, and it contains the essential elements and themes of Christian worship.

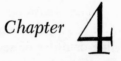

The Fourth to Ninth Centuries: The Radical Development of Christian Worship

THROUGHOUT the second and third centuries, Christian worship was relatively brief and austere. The regular Sunday service of the Holy Eucharist had definite shape and drama; it also had theological content together with ceremonial, color, and music. Yet the service was done briefly and without ostentation.

From the fourth century, however, and onward into the Middle Ages, vast—even radical—development characterized the worship of the Church. In the earlier centuries, action had been the emphasis in worship, but now many lengthy prayers and elaborate musical parts were added to the services. Far-reaching developments took place in the theology of worship as well as in liturgical ceremonial. The three chief causes of these radical developments in the Church's worship were the peace of the Church beginning in the fourth century, the theological controversies of the fourth and fifth centuries, and the breakup of the Roman Empire.

The Peace of the Church

The peace of the Church, which began in 313 during the reign of Emperor Constantine, had an astounding effect upon the whole life and institution of the Church. Christianity became a lawful religion for the first time, and, beginning with Constantine, all the emperors except one showed great favor to the Church. Thus, by the end of the fourth century, through custom and by law, Christianity was becoming the only accepted religion. Both the pagan religions and Judaism were being proscribed and repressed. The Church's favored, even exclusive, position brought her into close contact with the state, which further affected Christian life and worship. For example, the growing separation of clergy and laity, begun in the third century, was accelerated because of the great separation between the Roman state, especially the emperor, and the ordinary citizenry. At worship, especially in the Eastern part of the Church, ceremonial, color, and pageantry from the emperor's court were adapted for use in the services.

The major effect of this peace upon worship involved the new public image and atmosphere of Christianity. No longer did Christians have to meet secretly for a brief service of worship. Christianity was now a lawful religion, and the Church's worship could become an open matter. This new atmosphere encouraged the Church to create longer and much more colorful services. A very significant factor for liturgical change, because of the new public atmosphere, was the development of the distinctive church building. The Church no longer needed private houses or the small type of building used in the third century. Now great edifices, called basilicas, could be built. The building of great churches became a philanthropic activity of Christian emperors and wealthy lay people.

A splendid church demanded also a splendid service. Large silver patens now held the communion bread, and gold flagons the wine and water. The altar, formerly a movable table made usually of wood, was in Constantine's great basilicas made of gold and set in a fixed position. During this time the vestments of the clergy, specifically the alb and chasuble, continued to resemble the ordinary street clothes of any man in the empire as they had since the first century, but additions were being made from the fashion of dress at the imperial court. The clergy began to wear the stole, a badge of honor at state functions, and the maniple, a ceremonial handkerchief. Moreover, although Christians had bowed or knelt at the name of Jesus since New Testament times, now more bowing and kneeling was added to the service from the ceremonial of the imperial court.

Splendid worship in a splendid building demanded not only better appointments, vestments, and ceremony, but more content to the service. The earlier Church had emphasized action with few prayers in the Sunday service. Now more actions, musical parts, and lengthy prayers were added. Prayers were added to the service at the offertory (formerly a simple action of placing bread and wine on the altar), at the fraction (formerly a simple action of breaking the bread after the Eucharistic Prayer), at the time of Communion, and after Communion.

New and enduring elements which were added to the fourth-century service are revealed in two contemporary documents: the service used about mid-century by an Egyptian bishop named Serapion and an anonymous writing of the late fourth century from the Church of Antioch called *The Apostolic Constitutions*. Both documents show that the Sanctus (Holy, Holy, Holy) had been added to the service between the Sursum Corda (Lift up your hearts) and the Eucharistic Prayer. What Episcopalians usually call the "Grace" (or Minor Benediction) at the end of the Morning Prayer service—"The grace of our Lord Jesus Christ, and the love of God . . ."—appears as a fixed prayer in the service described by *The Apostolic Constitutions*. The great length of most of the prayers well illustrates the new atmosphere of Christian worship. In Bishop Serapion's Eucharistic Prayer, there is the usual recital of Jesus' words and acts at the Last Supper. After the Lord's words over the bread and before his words over the chalice, however, the bishop intruded a long prayer. In addition, the Eucharistic Prayer of *The Apostolic Constitutions* begins with a long summary of the Old Testament.

The preliminary, or Ante-Communion, part of the service was expanded also. At a regular Sunday service before the fourth century, Scripture lessons, interspersed with the singing of Psalms, and a sermon formed the preliminary part before the Communion proper. Now prayers and hymns such as the Gloria in Excelsis are added to this preliminary part of the service. A very important addition takes place with the entrance of the clergy at the very beginning of the service. The clergy entrance becomes a procession through the church with the singing of Psalms, the clergy being preceded by incense and candles in a manner similar to the entrance of the emperor and other high state officials.

These developments in Christian worship, resulting from the peace of the Church and the new status of Christianity, should be seen largely as developments in decoration and enrichment. The basic shape and character of the service established before the fourth century had not been changed. The basic elements of the preliminary part of the service were still the Scripture lessons, Psalms, and sermon. The Eucharist proper still had the basic shape of offertory, Eucharistic Prayer, fraction (breaking the bread), and Communion.

The decorative enrichment of the service in the fourth century and beyond, which involved added prayers, musical parts, ceremonies, and ornamentation, should not be considered as wrong, however, and today we should be careful not to condemn it. The Church of the fourth century was going into the entire Roman world. If the Church was to Christianize this world, she needed to be in touch with it, understand it, and meet its needs. These additions and enrichments were necessary to perform that task. The only question we should raise concerns whether or not these fourth-century decorative enrichments, some of which remain in our services, are understood today and are meeting the needs of our world.

The Theological Controversies

At the beginning of the fourth century, the prayers in the service were composed by each bishop, the celebrant. The prayers would reflect the theological themes which had become standard throughout the Church. By the end of the century the prayers of the Eucharist were becoming fixed in wording and in written form. One reason for this change was that the peace of the Church had caused many people to convert from paganism to Christianity. Peace and a favored position allowed free preaching of the gospel and easy exposure of people to the Church's doctrine. These conditions naturally attracted many converts. Sometimes, of course, pagans became Christians because the state was favoring the Church, and becoming a Christian was consequently the thing to do. But whatever their motivation, great numbers of people were flocking into the Church, and therefore a single Christian congregation in each city or town became impossible. Additional churches or congregations had to be established in different parts of cities and towns, and in the smaller towns and villages away from larger centers of population. No longer, therefore, could the bishop remain the chief officiant at the eucharistic service to which all Christians in an area came for worship. He now had to send presbyters out to the new congregations in the cities, towns, and rural areas, and he had to delegate to these presbyters his authority to be the president at the Eucharist.

There were, however, very few standards or rules concerning the education of the clergy in the early Church; some, therefore, were poorly educated. In order that such presbyters would use grammatically correct and well-constructed prayers at the services, the bishops began to make available to the presbyters their own prayers in written form for use at the Church's worship. The bishops did not have to be concerned about the preaching of the presbyters, for until the sixth century, usually only the bishop preached sermons at public worship. It is true that very gifted clergy such as Chrysostom and Augustine preached when they were still presbyters, but they were rare exceptions.

An even greater problem for the bishops than grammar was that of sound doctrine in the prayers. This was a vital concern, for theological controversy was not absent from the Church in the fourth and fifth centuries, and, consequently, the bishops had to make certain that the presbyters under their authority would employ correct doctrine in the prayers. Yet the only way to assure this was, again, for the bishops to authorize definite written prayers for use in all congregations. Thus, by the end of the fourth century, the content of the prayers was becoming fixed. The basic outline of the service had been standardized throughout the Church in the second century, but it was not until the end of the fourth century that the full content of worship evolved into authorized, set forms.

Theological controversies greatly affected the development of Christian worship not only in the fourth and fifth centuries but throughout the Church's history. In fact, the same controversies—the fourth-century dispute about the doctrine of the Trinity and the fifth-century battles over the Person of Christ, his divine and human natures—are causing upheaval in the churches today.

In the regular Sunday service the theological controversies made their greatest impact on the main prayer of the service, the Eucharistic Prayer, and on the laity's approach to receiving Communion. In the fourth century the Eucharistic Prayer changed from the primitive Church's idea of a prayer of thanksgiving or prayer of blessing to a prayer of consecration. The emphasis in this prayer came to be centered on the bread and wine's becoming the sacramental Body and Blood of Christ. The main theological question concerned time. *When* in the prayer, at *what moment,* does the change from bread and wine to sacramental form take place? Theologically, the problem is called the moment of consecration. We should note that the Church was not yet concerned about *how* the bread and wine became the Body and Blood of Christ. That was a question for the theologians of the Middle Ages. The fourth and fifth centuries were concerned with *when.*

For the Church in the western part of the Roman Empire, this moment of consecration occurred in the Eucharistic Prayer when the celebrant recited the words of institution from the Last Supper. When the celebrant pronounced Jesus' words, "This is my Body . . . This is my Blood," the natural elements were transformed into sacramental elements, according to the doctrine developed in the Western

Church. Actually, this concept of the moment of consecration developed in the West from the fourth century onward mainly because of the impetus given to the idea in the eastern part of the Church.

Before the end of the fourth century, the writings of Bishops Cyril of Jerusalem and John Chrysostom of Constantinople as well as *The Apostolic Constitutions* all attest to a fully developed concept of the moment of consecration in the Eastern Church. The actual moment differed in the East and the West, for in the Eastern Church, until this day, the moment of consecration is believed to be at the invocation of the Holy Spirit (the *epiclesis*) in the Eucharistic Prayer. John Chrysostom wrote, "The priest stands before the table holding up his hands to heaven and calling on the Holy Ghost to come and touch the elements." We have already seen in the third-century Eucharistic Prayer of Hippolytus that the *epiclesis,* or invocation of the Holy Spirit, was made to bless the Church's offering of bread and wine and to bless the people that they might be worthy to receive the Communion. By the end of the fourth century, however, the main emphasis of the *epiclesis* was to invoke the Holy Spirit upon the bread and wine in order that these elements would become, at that moment, the Body and Blood of Christ.

This concern with the moment of consecration effected a change in the order of service. The intercessory prayers, which had come before the offertory in the preliminary part of the service, were now put into the Eucharistic Prayer. Intercessory prayer became a new theme in the Prayer of Consecration. The Church made the change because she believed that her prayers for the living and the dead would be more effectual if they came at the holiest time of the service.

The new theological emphasis on the moment of consecration also radically altered the Church's whole approach to receiving Communion. The receiving of Holy Communion as the dramatic and natural climax of the sacramental meal was overshadowed by the Prayer of Consecration, during which the bread and wine became the Body and Blood of Christ. Christ's presence—as the host at the divine banquet, or through *anamnesis*—paled and gave way to belief in an extremely localized presence of the Lord in the bread and wine after the moment of consecration. No longer was the Eucharist a joyful service of thanksgiving; it had become a service full of mystery, fear, and awe. Bishops Cyril of Jerusalem and John Chrysostom of Constantinople refer to the Eucharist as the "awful and holy sacrifice," and the time when the service takes place as the "awful hour."

One of the consequences of this new theology was the addition of some prayers to the service after the Prayer of Consecration and before the people's Communion. These pre-communion devotions were added to make the people better prepared and more worthy to receive Holy Communion. The Lord's Prayer came into the service at this point as such a pre-communion devotion. The services described by Bishop Serapion and *The Apostolic Constitutions* show another prayer before Communion called the inclination prayer. The bishop turned to the people just before Communion, reaching his hands out over them as they bowed, and he prayed that they might be worthy. The Prayer of Humble Access (We do not presume to come to this thy Table, etc.) in the Prayer Book service is the same type of pre-communion prayer for worthiness.

The theological developments and accompanying liturgical additions of the fourth and fifth centuries increased so much the awe and mystery of the service that the lay people became discouraged, even inhibited, from receiving Communion. So much emphasis was placed upon the realistic presence of Christ in the bread and wine and so much preparation and worthiness was demanded of the laity that they refrained from coming to the altar at communion time. By the fifth century in the Eastern Church and the ninth century in the Western Church, the regular reception of Holy Communion at the Sunday service had become exceptional rather than normal.

Further consequences of these developments in eucharistic theology were the sharp separation of the clergy from the laity and the altar from the congregation. Although the separation of clergy and laity began before the fourth century, it was accentuated by the implications and results of theological emphasis on the moment of consecration. Only the celebrant (bishop or presbyter) had the power to consecrate the bread and wine, to recite the words of institution and invoke the Holy Spirit; only he could handle and distribute the awful, sacred elements.

The celebrant's position at the altar changed also. In the primitive Church, the celebrant faced the congregation across the altar table as the presiding officer at the banquet. The new theology and its resultant separation of clergy and laity caused the celebrant to come around the altar table and preside at the service with his back to the people. Now, the action at the altar was so holy that it should not be too visible. In order to make unmistakable the holiness of the action and the separation of clergy and altar from the people, the Western Church began to erect an open screen between the altar area (the sanctuary) and the nave of the church, where the people were. The screen was only symbolic since the people could see the priest and altar. The Eastern Church went to greater lengths to close off the sacred action and the clergy from the people. Beginning with the fifth century, Eastern churches were putting up first opaque cloth veils, then movable bronze screens, and eventually fixed screens of solid masonry so the people would not be able to see the celebrant consecrate the bread and wine. This solid screen, later known as the *iconostasis*, had three doors in it which were closed during the Prayer of Consecration. The *icono-stasis* remains a fixed element in the Eastern Orthodox churches to this day.

The liturgical movement in our day has sought to remove some of the barriers of separation between clergy and altar and the congregation. Thus, in many churches the altar has been moved out from the wall nearer to, or even in the midst of, the congregation. The celebrant has become once again the presiding officer at the banquet by facing the people across the altar table. The Church continues, however, to ponder and to struggle with the theological and liturgical elements in our services which not only separate clergy and laity but which inhibit the joy and thanksgiving that should characterize our worship.

THE BREAKUP OF THE ROMAN EMPIRE

The political division of the Roman Empire took place near the end of the third century under Emperor Diocletian, but even before that time the Christian Church was dividing into Eastern and Western Christendom because of cultural, linguistic, and theological differences. The Eastern Church was Greek in her language and thought; she had great interest in philosophy, speculative theology, and mysticism. The emphasis for the Greek East in theology and worship was upon the risen Lord Christ of eternity. The Western Church by the third century was Latin in language and thought. She showed little interest in philosophy and speculative theology. Her main concern centered in the administrative and judicial life of the Church. Since the early Latin theologians such as Tertullian and Cyprian had been trained in law, Western theology was usually expressed in terse legalistic definitions. The passion and death of Christ occupied the basic theological interest of the Western Church.

In the fifth century and afterward, the breakup of the Roman Empire continued because of divisions within the two spheres of East and West. Egypt and Syria seceded from the Eastern Empire for nationalistic and theological reasons. By the seventh century these countries had been conquered by the Moslems and had become part of the Islamic Empire. The Western Empire was rent asunder by the invasions of various tribes—the so-called barbarians—from Asia and from the eastern and northern parts of Europe. The Ostrogoths and then the Lombards invaded and conquered part of Italy; the Visigoths conquered and settled in Spain; the Franks and Burgundians went into Gaul (France); and the Vandals took North Africa.

This further partitioning of the old homogeneous Roman Empire had a significant effect on the development of Christian worship. While in relative isolation from each other, these various national and tribal states altered the form, content, and meaning of the services because of local needs and interests. In fact, each new area developed its own liturgical rite. The Church in Egypt, Christians in various parts of Syria, and the Orthodox Church of the eastern Roman Empire developed their own distinctive services. The Eastern Orthodox Church actually developed four eucharistic services, or liturgies: the Liturgy of St. Chrysostom (named for, but not created by, the famous bishop), which is used at most services during the year, and the Liturgies of St. Basil, St. James, and the Pre-Sanctified, which are used on special occasions.

All the Eastern liturgies went through extensive and radical development in the fourth and fifth centuries. However, they became quite stabilized in the sixth century, and by the eighth century they were so rigidly fixed that they have not changed even today.

Western Christian patterns of worship did not develop

so swiftly, nor did they become rigid, as did the Eastern. In fact, one cannot really speak of a fixed worship in the West until the Reformation of the sixteenth century. The establishment of tribal states in Western Europe in the fifth and sixth centuries helped to create several distinct Western liturgies. They were the Milanese, or Ambrosian, rite of northern Italy, the Mozarabic rite of Spain, the Gallican rite of Gaul, the Celtic rite of Ireland and Scotland, and the Roman rite of the Church in the city of Rome and throughout central Italy.

By 1100, however, all these liturgies except one had dropped from common use or had been displaced by the one exception—the Roman rite. The Roman liturgy became and has remained the basic service of Western Christendom since the twelfth century. Most non-Roman Catholic worship, especially the Episcopal and Lutheran services, has been greatly influenced by the Roman liturgy.

The services of the Church of Rome came to be accepted by all Christians in Western Europe for several reasons. Certainly the authoritative ascendancy of the Church and pope of Rome over Western Christendom from the third century onward was a major factor. Moreover, in Western Europe from the fifth to the eleventh century, so many agonizing upheavals occurred politically, economically, and socially that Western man could find but one source of hope and unity— the Church, especially the Church of Rome. Nevertheless, it is highly significant that although all the areas of Western Christendom came to feel they should adopt the worship of the Roman Church, neither the pope nor the Church of Rome forced services on the rest of Western Christendom. It was not until 1570, well into the Reformation period, that Pope Pius V decreed the Roman rite to be the standard liturgy for the Roman Catholic Church.

It is a startling revelation to many non-Roman Catholic Christians today to learn that the services of the Church of

Rome in the early medieval period were the most austere and least elaborate of all the Western liturgies. Much of the lavish ceremonial and many of the elaborate, lengthy services which are sometimes associated with Roman Catholic worship came originally from the Gallican and Mozarabic services. These regional liturgies did not fade away suddenly; they made their influence felt upon the Roman service, which was displacing them. The Gallican rite, for example, made some distinctive contributions to the Roman service. The prayers of the Gallican services were wordy, full of repetition and rhetorical flourishes. This was in great contrast to the terse Latin prayers of the Roman rite. Some of this Gallican wordiness made its way into the collects and Eucharistic Prayer of the Roman rite and through that service into the Book of Common Prayer. Much of the elaborate Gallican ceremonial was eventually incorporated into the Roman services. The use of ashes on Ash Wednesday, palms on Palm Sunday, and many Holy Week ceremonies were either Gallican in origin or were first used in the West in the Gallican liturgy, having been adopted from Eastern rites.

THE ROMAN SERVICE

Since the eucharistic service of the Church of Rome is the chief source for the service of the Holy Communion in the Book of Common Prayer, attention should be given to that service as it appeared about 900. The change and development of the service from the relatively brief service of action as described seven hundred years before in *The Apostolic Tradition* of Hippolytus is most revealing.

The service began with the choir and congregation singing the introit psalm while the clergy proceeded from their vesting room (usually near the rear door) to the altar. The clergy would be preceded by acolytes carrying candles and swinging incense pots. Although candles and incense were also used in Hebrew worship, this particular ceremonial came

from the ancient secular concept of honor in the imperial
court, where emperors, magistrates, and most important officials were preceded by lights and incense.

After singing the introit the congregation and choir would
sing the Kyrie Eleison (Lord have mercy). This Kyrie was,
and in the Prayer Book service still is, a relic from the intercessory litany of the early church service. In the earlier period, when the intercessory prayers came just before the
offertory, the deacon called out biddings for various subjects,
the congregation then prayed silently, and the celebrant
summed up their silent intercessions with a short collect. As
time went on, the people's silent prayers were replaced by a
congregational cry of "Kyrie eleison" to each bidding of the
deacon. The biddings and responses evolved into an intercessory litany. Such litanies still abound in the liturgy of the
Eastern Orthodox Church.

The Kyrie had a different history in the West. Toward the
end of the sixth century, in an effort to shorten the eucharistic service on weekdays, Pope Gregory I deleted the deacon's intercessory biddings and simply had the congregation
sing the Kyrie response. By 900 the intercessory biddings had
dropped out of all services, and only the singing of the Kyrie
remained. In order to give variety to the Kyrie, the Western
Church developed a ninefold pattern of singing "Kyrie eleison" (Lord have mercy) three times, "Christe eleison"
(Christ have mercy) three times, and then "Kyrie eleison"
three times again.

We ought to note that the Greek phrase *Kyrie eleison*
is not a penitential cry as it appears to be in Western services. In Greek it means "Lord be good [or be kind] to us,"
for it was a response to a bidding in an intercessory litany.

The service's choral beginning continued after the introit
and Kyrie with the singing of the Gloria in Excelsis (Glory
be to God on high) on Sundays and special feast days. Orig-

inally the Gloria in Excelsis was an Eastern hymn which was brought to the West at an early time and made a permanent part of the service in the sixth century. The Gloria in the beginning of the service emphasized the festive note of the Eucharist, that it was a service of joy and thanksgiving.

Until about 900 this choral beginning was set to simple and well-known music and was sung by both congregation and choir. After 900, however, the Western Church developed elaborate choir music which greatly inhibited the congregation from taking its long-established part in the service. By the twelfth century all the choral parts of the service were sung exclusively by either the clergy or the choir.

The ancient and basic part of the Ante-Communion, the Scripture lessons, followed the Gloria in Excelsis. Although the Roman service originally had an Old Testament lesson, by 900 only the New Testament Epistle and Gospel lessons remained in the service. Between these lessons the choir and congregation sang a gradual psalm, and the Gospel procession took place just before the singing of the Gospel lesson. As early as the fourth century the Roman Church had emphasized the importance of the Gospel lesson by having acolytes with torches precede the deacon to the head of the nave or into the pulpit, where he would sing the Gospel lesson. As in early times the sermon followed the Scripture lessons.

There was no creed in the Roman service of 900; it was not put into the Mass in Rome until 1014. The first time a creed appeared in the Church's worship was in an Eastern service about 510 A.D. The Patriarch of Constantinople at the time was suspected of heresy, and in order to prove his orthodoxy he had the Nicene Creed put into the service. Since the Greeks conquered part of Spain in the sixth century and took some of their liturgical ideas with them, the Spanish, or Mozarabic, rite added the Nicene Creed to the Eucharist in 589. Eventually the Gallican rite copied the idea from the

Mozarabic service. In 1014 the German Emperor Henry II, who in Germany had been accustomed to a Gallicanized Roman service with the creed, captured Rome. As Henry worshiped in the churches of the city of Rome, he became disappointed that the creed was not sung in the Roman service. His strong suggestion that it be added to the Roman service was soon heeded by Pope Benedict VIII.

In the Roman service, the Eucharist proper began, as always, with the offertory. Although by 900 the lay people were not receiving Communion very often, the ancient Roman custom of having an offertory procession still prevailed. While a psalm was sung, the officiating clergy went to the nave and choir, received loaves of bread and flagons of wine, proceeded to the altar, and placed the gifts upon it.

The offertory was followed by the traditional introduction to the Eucharistic Prayer, an introduction which had been expanded from earlier times. After the ancient greeting (The Lord be with you) and Sursum Corda (Lift up your hearts), a preface had been inserted in order to add a seasonal note at this point. Then came the ancient Sanctus (Holy, Holy, Holy), followed by another addition, the Benedictus qui Venit (Blessed is he who comes in the Name of the Lord), which the Roman Church had adopted from the Gallican service.

After this lengthy introduction, there followed the Eucharistic Prayer, now understood to be a prayer of consecration during which the bread and wine became the Body and Blood of Christ. As has been mentioned, the intercessions were added to the prayer in the fourth century. The Roman Prayer of Consecration had all the ancient and basic themes as mentioned by *The Apostolic Tradition* except the *epiclesis* or invocation of the Holy Spirit, which remained an essential theme in the Eastern service. As we shall see, Anglican interest in Eastern liturgies was responsible for that Church's adopting an *epiclesis* in its Prayer Book service.

The pre-communion devotions which followed the Eucharistic Prayer began with the Lord's Prayer, added to the service by Pope Gregory I. Then after the traditional fraction, or breaking of the bread, the Roman service had the kiss of peace. Although all other Eastern and Western liturgies to that time had the kiss of peace before or after the offertory, the Roman service placed it in this unique position before Communion. By 900 the pre-communion devotions had been further expanded with the Agnus Dei (O Lamb of God), a Syrian hymn put into the service by a Greek-speaking pope about 700. Then followed the administration of Holy Communion.

In 900 the Roman service still had a brief conclusion similar to that of the early Church. After Communion came a short collect praying for a worthy life for the communicants. This was followed by the closing dismissal, "Ite, missa est," which literally means, "Go, you are dismissed," but which the Roman Catholic Church today translates as, "Go, Mass is ended," because the Roman term for the service—Mass—comes from the dismissal word *missa*.

The service of 900 contained many additions—some necessary, some superfluous—to the third-century service of *The Apostolic Tradition*. Yet the basic shape and essential themes of the service of the early Church still remained. The Roman service was the briefest in order and content and the least elaborate in ceremonial of all the Christian liturgies of that day. It was this conservative and relatively austere Roman service which became the basis for the service of the Holy Communion in the Book of Common Prayer.

Chapter 5

The Middle Ages

THE MIDDLE AGES initiated some exciting things in the history of Western man. The beginnings of modern democratic institutions, capitalism, and scientific research took place in the medieval period. In church history during this period, the greatest devotional classics of Christianity were written, and most magnificent advances in Christian art and architecture were made. Unfortunately, though, one cannot be exuberant about the history of Christian worship in the Middle Ages. A fair verdict would be that Christian liturgy suffered a decline.

Most of the problem with Christian worship in the Middle Ages was theological. In the fourth century and after, the Church had become concerned about the moment of consecration in the Eucharist. By the ninth century the Western Church's concern had changed to *how* Christ was present in the bread and wine. Theological debate on this question continued for centuries. Finally, at the Lateran Council of 1215, the Church decided she knew how Christ was present, and Transubstantiation was made the official doctrine of the Church.

The doctrine of Transubstantiation, which is officially held today in the West only by the Roman Catholic Church, declares that after the celebrant has recited the words of institution in the Prayer of Consecration, the bread and wine truly and substantially become the Body and Blood of Christ under the outward signs of bread and wine. The accidents, or outward forms, remain bread and wine, but the substance, or essence, is the Body and Blood of Christ.

Since the theologians and church leaders of the Middle Ages had such a fantastic penchant for understanding and explaining everything in minute detail, one can readily understand their development of the doctrine of Transubstantiation. The doctrine was based on the predominant medieval philosophy of realism, which took the substance and accidents of things very seriously. For the medieval mind, Transubstantiation was a proper explanation of a really unexplainable mystery: Christ's presence in Christian worship and sacrament. The basic problem with the doctrine has always involved the Church's belief about Christ himself. Since the divine and human natures of Christ are united in one Person, according to Transubstantiation the substance of his human nature as well as that of his divine nature must be present in the consecrated bread and wine. In fact, medieval theologians and preachers often stressed Christ's humanity in the sacrament—that the substance of his corporeal, or natural, Body and Blood, born of Mary, was present under the signs of bread and wine. This interpretation of Transubstantiation caused the Protestant reformers vehemently to reject the doctrine.

Another great problem today is that few people think,

speak, or understand anything in terms of substance and accidents. Moreover, many churchmen today have come to the more mature judgment that all of God's mysteries cannot be minutely explained. From the earliest days of the New Testament Church, Christians believed that the Lord Christ was present with them in eucharistic worship. The Lord's Supper was a foretaste of the Messianic Banquet, and the risen Lord was the unseen but real host of the Supper. Another tradition emphasized Christ's presence through *anamnesis*, the Church's objective recalling of the Lord's sacrificial death and resurrection. The Church did not go beyond these broad explanations until Christian philosophers and theologians became so extremely realistic and literal minded that ideas such as those of the moment of consecration and Transubstantiation had to develop in order to satisfy them. Our problem today is the delicate one of understanding intellectually and emotionally that our Lord is present in worship without encumbering this mystery with detailed theories as to precisely how, when, or in what manner, he is present.

Transubstantiation had a serious effect on Christian worship. Such a doctrine made reception of the sacrament of Communion even more solemn. The number of lay communions, which had been declining after the fifth century, declined even more. Some laymen would go years before they received the Holy Communion. In fact the very Lateran Council which in 1215 officially decreed Transubstantiation also had to decree that every communicant must receive the Holy Communion once a year. The doctrine also caused further separation between priest and people. The priest had the power, it was believed, to make the bread and wine into the Body and Blood of Christ by reciting the words of institution. As a result, the layman's role in the life of the Church was insignificant compared to that of the priest.

A further consequence involved the Prayer of Consecration, which became the most important part of eucharistic worship. The clergy believed this important prayer to be so holy that the congregation should not even hear it; therefore, the celebrant began to whisper the prayer. The result of all this was that the lay people lost all participation in the regular Sunday service. They had nothing to do; they did not even understand what was going on. The rise of choirs and elaborate church music kept them from participating in the choral parts; theological doctrine inhibited their receiving Communion; and the service was celebrated in a language many people did not understand. By the Middle Ages only the most educated people, of whom there were few, understood the Latin of the Church's worship. Most of the lay people spoke only their developing national languages—French, German, English, etc.

Western man likes to be active, however; therefore, something had to be devised for the congregation to do while the clergy and choir carried on the worship of the Church. Prayer beads and individual prayer books for the literate were created to keep the laity busy during the service. Congregational participation was reduced, therefore, to individual, private devotions. In order to alert the congregation to what was going on at the altar, particularly at the time of consecration, a bell was rung to gain their attention. Finally, by the thirteenth century, in order to emphasize the moment of consecration and the doctrine of Transubstantiation, the celebrant began to raise up a piece of bread (the large priest's Host) just after the words of institution. The laity liked this action so much that this elevation became a major part of eucharistic worship in the later Middle Ages. Since the laity rarely received the Holy Communion, gazing upon the elevated Host, whose substance was believed to be the Body of Christ, became a substitute for Communion.

The real tragedy in all this was that the lay people lost

not only their part but also any sense of participation in the public, corporate worship of the Church. They came to church to pray their own private devotions and to be spectators at the elevation of the Host. The concept of the Christian community gathered for corporate worship of God was lost.

The loss of this concept was perpetuated in the Protestant churches during and after the sixteenth-century Reformation. Although the Reformation churches believed they were reacting against the medieval Church in the matter of worship, they actually continued the medieval pattern under new forms. Protestant worship also shied away from the concept of the community at corporate worship and emphasized personal individualistic piety. The Sunday service, as we know, has long focused upon the minister, who preaches lengthy sermons and delivers lengthy prayers, while the people sit or kneel as spectators. The major effort of the liturgical movement in all the churches of our time has been to overcome the one-sided individualism of Christian worship in favor of true corporate worship, to lessen the emphasis on the priest or minister in corporate worship, and to reintroduce the congregation's essential participation in the public worship of the Church.

Medieval formulations of eucharistic sacrifice also seriously affected Christian worship. From earliest times the Church had looked upon the Eucharist as being in some sense a sacrifice. Yet the early Church did not rigidly define the eucharistic sacrifice. The Eucharist was a sacrifice because of the people's offering of bread and wine or their offering of praise and thanksgiving; or the Eucharist was a sacrifice because through *anamnesis* the sacrifice of Christ was objectively recalled.

After the fifth century, however, eucharistic sacrifice was almost exclusively linked to Christ's death because of the

Church's extremely realistic, even physical, approach to Christ's presence in the bread and wine. Since Christ was present in and under the signs of bread and wine, when the bread and cup were offered in the Prayer of Consecration, it was no longer bread and wine which were being offered, but Christ Himself. Hence, the emphasis now centered on offering Christ in the Eucharist. The Church's official doctrine and most reputable theologians never went beyond this idea that the eucharistic sacrifice consisted of the Church's offering of Christ's sacrifice to God. Some uncautious theologians, however, and especially parish clergy and laity came to believe that Christ was sacrificed anew at each Eucharist. In many ways these people cannot be blamed for their erroneous view. The Church's official teaching had so identified the Eucharist with Christ's death that it was very easy for unlearned clergy and laity to believe that Christ was repeatedly sacrificed at each Eucharist. A good example of this unfortunate development was that by the tenth century the communion bread was called the "Host" from the Latin *hostia*, which referred to the victim of a sacrifice.

Even more devastating to Christian doctrine and worship were the conclusions which the medieval Church drew from the new doctrine of eucharistic sacrifice. The main conclusion they drew was the doctrine of merit. From New Testament times, Christians had believed that Christ's one, true sacrifice of death and resurrection was meritorious and efficacious for all mankind. Through Christ's sacrifice, man's sins are forgiven, the separation between God and man is overcome and the relationship restored, and man is redeemed. In the Middle Ages, however, the idea developed that since Christ's sacrifice is offered in the Eucharist, the Eucharist must also offer merit and efficacy. Lay people paid the clergy to celebrate a private Eucharist in order to gain special merit or favor for the sick, the dying, for travelers, in order to win battles or have better harvests. Because of the medieval Church's tremendous interest in and fear of sin, death, purgatory, and hell, clergy and laity began to have eucharistic services offered for individual persons, living or dead, in order that the supposed merit gained from the service could be applied to the individual's time in purgatory. It is noteworthy that as early as the second century, the Church had offered the Holy Eucharist for departed Christians, but the whole meaning and atmosphere had been different in the early Church. At that time the Eucharist was celebrated in thanksgiving for the life of the departed and not to gain merit or time off in purgatory for the deceased. In the Middle Ages, however, wealthy laymen hired clergy to hold services for them every day, while the poor saved and saved to buy one service for themselves to reduce their time in purgatory.

These extraordinary developments in the idea of eucharistic sacrifice and merit theology created new kinds of eucharistic services. At the private service, or votive Mass, the priest did not need other sacred ministers such as deacons, nor did he need even choir or congregation. Thus, for the first time the service began to be said or read by the officiating minister. Before the thirteenth century the said service usually was limited to a weekday private service carried on by priest and acolyte with few or no lay people in the congregation. The Sunday service attended by all Christians remained a completely sung Eucharist with choir and other clergy assisting the celebrant. By the thirteenth century the lay people began more and more to attend the private said service, or Low Mass, as it was called. This service, read rapidly and with no sermon, was over quickly, and the layman did not have to spend much time at a service he did not understand or in which he had no part. All the layman had to do was to make some private devotions and gaze upon the elevated Host. Throughout the later Middle Ages on Sundays,

many parish churches had a fully sung Eucharist with elaborate ceremonial, called a High Mass, but all churches had
the brief said, or Low, Mass, which many lay people attended. Without music or color, with no participation and
little understanding of what was going on, the Church's
worship reached its lowest ebb in the medieval Low Mass.

Brief mention should be made of three aspects of medieval worship which affected Reformation and modern
Christian worship. Although the said service, or Low Mass,
reduced the time needed for worship, the medieval Church
also added parts to the service, especially at the beginning
and at the end. The extremely realistic emphasis upon a
physical Christ present at the service, and the concomitant
emphasis on man's sin and need for worthiness, caused the
Church to attach a lengthy penitential preparation to the
beginning of the service. Conducted strictly by priest and
acolyte, the congregation kneeling in silence, this preparation consisted of confession and penitential prayers and
Psalms. This medieval penitential beginning has affected all
Christian worship ever since.

The end of the service was also elaborated in the Middle
Ages. After Communion, long prayers and canticles of thanksgiving and prayers for more worthiness were added along
with a blessing of the people. The later medieval additions
of long thanksgivings, other prayers, canticles, and the blessing have continued in our services today.

The addition of superfluous ceremonies, most of them
from the Gallican territories of France and Germany, also
characterized medieval worship. For example, there was the
ceremonial washing, or lavabo. In the early Church the
presiding officiant at the Eucharist washed his hands after
the offertory and before the Eucharistic Prayer. This practice
came from the Hebrew idea that one should wash before
prayer. The medieval Church became obsessed with cere-

monial cleansings, however. Thus, the celebrant had to wash
his hands before vesting; the people had to be washed cere-
monially before the service, and so an acolyte came out at
the beginning of the service and sprinkled them (this is
called the Asperges); also holy-water stoups were placed
at the church door for people to wash themselves symbolically as they entered and left the church. The tragedy of the
superfluous additions was that they overemphasized some
very ancient and fine ceremonies of Christian worship.

The medieval Church also developed an excessive use of
candles and incense. Like the lavabo, candles and incense
had been used in church services from earliest times for
clergy and Gospel processions. Church use of them was
derived from both the Hebrews and the Greeks. In the
Middle Ages the Church increased greatly the number of
candles employed and the occasions in the service when
candles and incense would be used.

The Reformation churches reacted strongly against these
excessive ceremonies and almost completely eliminated them.
For good reason these new churches failed to understand
that lavabo, incense, and candle were part of the Church's
primitive worship, and when used sparingly and properly
could add significant meaning and color to Christian worship.

We must not completely despair of Christian worship in
the Middle Ages, for there were some clergy, chiefly in
France and Germany, who were genuinely concerned about
the laity's plight in the matter of corporate worship. They
recognized that the congregation had no part in the public
worship, but were mere spectators. Thus, in some areas of
France and Germany, clergy began to try to involve the
laity by adding a congregational part to the service. After
the sermon at the High Mass on Sundays and great festivals,
the clergy held a brief service called Prone in the native
tongue of the people.

Although the content of this Prone vernacular service differed from place to place, some or all of the following might be included in it: intercessory prayers, Psalms, the Lord's Prayer, Hail Mary, Apostles' Creed, Decalogue (Ten Commandments), General Confession and Absolution, and a brief instruction on one of these parts. Prone had significant effect upon worship in the Reformation churches, for the reformers demanded that corporate worship be in the native tongue and that there be frequent use of the Decalogue and the General Confession.

In its theological formulations, its said services, its penitential additions to the service, its elaboration of ceremonies, and its experiments in a vernacular service, the medieval Church has greatly influenced our worship today.

Chapter 6

The Reformation and After

THE PROTESTANT REFORMATION of the sixteenth century stands out in the history of Western Christianity as a time of excitement, revolution, and creativity. In rending asunder the rigid outlook of the later medieval Church, the reformers did not offer merely a single alternative to traditional Christianity but rather a variety of alternatives. Once the medieval Church had begun to be challenged successfully by the German monk Martin Luther in the second decade of the sixteenth century, scores of other concerned and thoughtful churchmen tried their hand at reforming the "old Church." Therefore, Western Christians were offered a wide variety of new doctrines—especially concerning the Church, sacraments, and priesthood—as well as new forms of ministry and church government.

In the matter of Christian worship, however, the Protestant reformers present an enigma, even a paradox. For although they did initiate changes in the nature and forms of Christian worship, some of which have influenced Protestantism to this day, the reformers really had little interest in liturgy. With the exception of the English Reformation, which will be treated separately, rarely did the reformers evidence the kind of creativity in worship that they did in Christian doctrine and church government.

The reformers' lack of creative interest in worship can be attributed chiefly to their preoccupation with doctrine and church government. Their primary concern was to reform the medieval understanding of Church, sacraments, and ministry as well as the government of the Church. Since worship is integral to one's view of Church, sacraments, and ministry, it had to be dealt with, but it remained a secondary concern. Moreover, all the reformers believed that the Holy Scriptures and not the Church, the bishops, or the pope should be the highest authority in matters of doctrine, liturgy, and church government. Yet as we have seen in Chapter 1, the New Testament, for various reasons, does not provide us with precise liturgical forms. When this lack of preciseness combined with the reformers' zeal for the literal word of the Bible, liturgy was bound to occupy a secondary position.

Nevertheless, the reformers' approach to worship was very much in tune with the later medieval Church, which exhibited the same lack of enthusiasm for the corporate worship of the Christian community. Although the reformers reacted against medieval Christianity, they had been reared in it and were often influenced by it. As we have noted and shall presently develop in detail, one of the extraordinary similarities between medieval and Protestant worship was their emphasis upon the clergyman in corporate worship, with little or no congregational involvement.

MARTIN LUTHER

Martin Luther, the father of the Protestant Reformation, illustrates well the reformers' general lack of creativity in liturgical worship. On the Eve of All Saints in 1517, Luther began his assault on the medieval Church by nailing his famous Ninety-five Theses to the door of the Castle Church in Wittenberg, Germany. Not until almost six years later, however, did he make his first attempt at liturgical reforms. Luther's primary concern was doctrine: stressing the Scriptures and the doctrines of justification by faith and the priesthood of all believers against the medieval understanding of Church and ministry.

In the matter of sacraments, Luther was more conservative. In accord with traditional Christianity, he strongly believed the sacraments to be a means of God's grace to man. Concerning the sacrament of the altar, he did denounce the medieval understanding of eucharistic sacrifice as implying a repeated sacrifice of Christ; he also denied vehemently that any merit could be gained from votive or private masses. Yet he did not altogether overthrow the idea of eucharistic sacrifice. He maintained that the Christian offers himself and his praise and thanksgiving to the Lord in the sacramental service of the altar.

Luther's approach to the presence of Christ in the eucharistic elements was the most conservative of all the Protestant reformers. He denied the medieval doctrine of Transubstantiation, but he strongly advocated a localized realistic presence of Christ in the sacramental elements of bread and wine. Unlike the medieval Church, Luther did not precisely define his doctrine of eucharistic presence, but insisted that the matter remained a mystery known only to God. He did stress Christ's ubiquity, however—that the Lord could be present everywhere and was truly present in his full nature in the consecrated bread and wine.

The German reformer's conservative approach to sacraments no doubt influenced his approach to the worship of the
Church. In one significant sense Luther made no departure
from the Sunday worship of traditional Christianity. He
always believed that the chief form of Christian worship
should be the Eucharist, or Mass. For weekdays Luther advocated and helped develop a service based on the reading
and preaching of the Word of God as revealed in Holy
Scripture, which was to educate the people in true doctrine;
but the Sunday service was always to be the Lord's Supper,
with sermon.

When by 1523 some of his disciples, notably Andreas
Carlstadt, had begun to make radical changes in the traditional service, Luther felt compelled to publish his own
ideas for Sunday worship. His first liturgical effort, called
Formula Missae, was a rather conservative revision of the
traditional Roman Mass. The service remained in Latin,
and much of the ceremonial, incense, and vestments of the
old service were retained at least as options. Luther did
radically change two parts of the service which he believed
had led to erroneous doctrines, namely the offertory and the
Prayer of Consecration. Medieval theologians had used these
two parts of the service to substantiate their views of eucharistic sacrifice, merit, and Transubstantiation. Therefore,
the German reformer completely eliminated the offertory and
had the bread and wine prepared during the singing of the
Nicene Creed.

He reduced the Prayer of Consecration to the words of
institution, the recitation of the acts and words of Jesus at
the Last Supper. This severe truncation of the Eucharistic
Prayer was ordered not simply because the old prayer led
to erroneous doctrine but also because for Luther the Word
of God was the only true and authoritative force in all life.
Christ was the Word of God; His words and acts were
recorded in Scripture, which itself then could be called the

Word of God. Since the scriptural accounts of the Last Supper emphasized almost exclusively Jesus' words and acts, Luther believed that these words of institution were sufficient to consecrate the bread and wine.

Luther's first attempt at liturgical reform hardly met the needs of the German reform movement. It was too conservative; it was still in Latin and not in the language of the people. Moved, therefore, by the continuing radical experiments of his disciples in other parts of Germany, Luther devised a German service, *Deutsche Messe,* which he used for a year at his church in Wittenberg before publishing it in 1526. Although not slavishly copied in detail, Luther's *Deutsche Messe* became the model for all Lutheran churches from the sixteenth century to the present time. The service was to be in the vernacular; the context remained the Mass, or Lord's Supper; and some ceremonies such as the elevation of the consecrated Host at the words of institution were retained, as were vestments, candles, and altar. The outline of the service continued to follow the Roman rite except that Luther persisted in his characteristic negative principle of expunging what he did not like in the old service. Thus, the preliminary, or Ante-Communion, remained intact except for deleting the Gloria in Excelsis, making the Kyrie threefold instead of ninefold, replacing the Nicene Creed with the Apostles' Creed, and appointing German hymns to be used in place of both the Latin Psalm introit at the beginning of the service and the Latin gradual between the Epistle and Gospel. Actually the one really creative contribution of Luther to liturgical worship was his use of popular vernacular hymns in the service. Of all the continental Protestant reformers, only Luther sought active participation of the congregation in the Church's worship through his emphasis on hymnody.

Luther's Communion, or Eucharist proper, was brief in content because of his propensity for deletion. Since he would allow no offertory, the Communion proper began with a paraphrase of the Lord's Prayer followed by an exhortation declaring the significance of the sacrament of Holy Communion. Then followed the recitation of the words of institution, during which Luther retained the elevation of the Host and the fraction. The distribution of Holy Communion followed immediately. As Luther interpreted the scriptural accounts, Jesus recited the words and then gave the bread and wine to his disciples; thus, the Church must also do this in order to follow exactly the Word of God. What Luther failed to understand was that the early Church had used Jesus' words and actions as the outline for the Communion proper. Jesus took bread, so the offertory; he blessed and broke it, so the Prayer of Consecration and the fraction; and he gave to his disciples, so the administration of Holy Communion.

Luther did allow the Sanctus and Agnus Dei from the old service, as well as German hymns, to be sung during the distribution of the sacrament. The service ended with the traditional post-communion collect and blessing, but for the blessing Luther prescribed the Aaronic form from the Old Testament (The Lord bless thee and keep thee, etc.) rather than the traditional formula (The blessing of God Almighty, etc.).

From the viewpoint of the history of Christian worship, Luther's liturgy can be criticized on two accounts. Since he reduced the Prayer of Consecration to Jesus' words of institution, he eliminated all the other traditional theological themes associated with the prayer. More particularly he eliminated the intercessory prayers, one of the essential liturgical themes in Christian worship, because the Roman Mass had incorporated the intercessions into the Eucharistic Prayer. Luther also stressed a pedagogical note in liturgy. Public worship began to become a major vehicle for instructing and edifying the congregation. The Communion proper

in Luther's service was strongly instructional with its para-
phrasing of the Lord's Prayer and its exhortation on the
meaning of Communion. He adopted these elements from the
medieval Prone service, which itself had a strong note of
instruction about faith and worship. Luther further emphasized the preaching of the Word of God (Christ as revealed
in the Scriptures), and because he had deleted many of the
traditional parts of the service, in proportion and length the
sermon came to dominate the Sunday service. For Luther,
as for all the reformers, preaching became the chief means
of teaching the new Protestant doctrines while at the same
time inveighing against the old religion.

In his teaching about the Lord's Supper, Luther frequently stressed the importance of Communion; in fact he
ruled that some or all of the congregation had to receive
the sacrament at each celebration. The problem was that the
laity had no tradition for receiving the sacrament regularly.
For almost a thousand years, Western lay Christians had
been receiving Holy Communion infrequently, for the pre-
ceding five hundred years usually only at Easter. Since
tradition proved too great a force and a medieval-like non-
communicating Eucharist became a real problem, Luther
established two liturgical principles concerning the Sunday
service. Those who wished to communicate had to inform
the minister before the service, and if no one signified an
intention to receive the sacrament, the minister was to
proceed with the service omitting the exhortation, words
of institution, Communion, and post-communion prayer. In
other words, the service was basically Ante-Communion
with a concluding blessing. This type of service soon became the norm for most Lutheran churches, except that in
larger churches and cathedrals, the whole liturgy usually
was done each Sunday because there were some communicants.

Perhaps because his interest was more doctrinal than

liturgical, Luther perpetuated and even enhanced the later medieval aspect of individualism in public corporate worship. Medieval worship inspired individualism because the service centered on the priest while the members of the congregation were left to offer their personal devotions. Luther's note of individualism came from his primary doctrinal emphasis on justification by faith in which he strongly asserted a personal faith relationship between God and the individual Christian. This doctrinal idea appeared in Luther's liturgy in the matter of reception of Communion. The individual had to signify to the minister his personal intention to receive the sacrament. Therefore, Communion became a strongly individual experience rather than the corporate act of the Christian community.

From a liturgical point of view, Luther may be criticized on many accounts: his basic negativism in dealing with the form and content of services; his deletion of intercessory prayer from the Sunday service; and his tendency to emphasize individualism and edification rather than the corporate offering of worship. However, one should not overlook Luther's positive contributions to Christian worship: he maintained the Eucharist as the primary service of Christian worship as it had been since New Testament times; he did not discard, but sought to reform, the traditional Christian doctrines of sacramental grace, eucharistic sacrifice, and the presence of Christ; and he recovered the early church emphasis upon Communion. In the services he finally came to demand the vernacular, and he sought to involve the congregation through popular evangelical hymnody.

Luther's negative and positive contributions to corporate worship influenced not only the Lutheran churches in Germany, Scandinavia, and central Europe; as will be seen, he and other Lutheran reformers were influential sources for the establishment of the Anglican liturgy in the Book of Common Prayer. In fact, if the more radical Swiss reformers had not risen up during Luther's lifetime and had not eventually won more allegiance in Europe and America than the father of the Reformation, no doubt Luther's liturgy would have become the basis for Protestant worship. But as history unfolded, the Swiss reformers—led by Zwingli of Zurich and Calvin in Geneva—became the primary force in the development of Protestantism.

ZWINGLI OF ZURICH

Soon after Luther began to challenge the medieval Church with his Ninety-five Theses, Huldreich Zwingli, a priest in Zurich, Switzerland, launched the more radical Swiss Reformation. By the early 1520's, Zwingli had organized the first Reformed church, from which would develop the influential and numerous Reformed churches, first throughout Europe, later in America, and today in all places of the world. Although he was the founder of this global form of Protestantism, Zwingli's contribution to the development of the Reformed tradition was limited because he died relatively early in the Reformation period during a religious war in 1531. Leadership of the Reformed tradition then passed to the Frenchman who became the Protestant apostle of Geneva, John Calvin.

In matters of doctrine, discipline, and government in the Protestant Reformed churches, Calvin had, and has continued to hold, the greatest influence. However, Zwingli did make one enduring contribution to the Reformed tradition in his approach to liturgy and worship. In fact, since the sixteenth century, Zwingli's approach to worship has in some degree affected all non-Roman Western churches, whether Reformed, Lutheran, Anglican, or Free. In the history of Christian worship, Zwingli is a person to be reckoned with.

Like Luther's, Zwingli's ideas on worship were a result of his theological beliefs. Yet unlike Luther's, Zwingli's doctrines were extremely radical and violently in opposition to traditional Christianity. Therefore, his resultant ideas on worship differed greatly from those of all previous centuries. Most later Protestants rejected Zwingli's theological doctrines, but paradoxically his ideas on worship were more and more accepted by them.

The chief teaching of Zwingli which so affected Protestant worship was his minimal view of sacraments. From his theological emphasis on the utter transcendence of God, who is spirit, Zwingli contended that material elements such as water and bread and wine could not be vehicles of God's grace. Therefore, the sacraments were not means of grace; they had no objective efficacy. He recognized, though, that the Scripture, which he held to be the supreme authority over the Church, did stress Baptism and the Lord's Supper; hence, he had to allow these traditional sacramental rites in his church. For him, Baptism and Holy Communion were merely pledges or signs (today we might use the term "visual aids") of what God had done through Christ for man long ago. They conveyed no further grace or forgiveness. When the Christian participated in these rites, especially the Lord's Supper, all he did was to demonstrate his faith and make a public testimony for the cause of Christ.

Zwingli's ideas about matter and spirit naturally had a strong effect on his approach to traditional eucharistic doctrines. Eucharistic sacrifice he rejected completely. Unlike Luther, Zwingli would not allow in his liturgical teaching or actual services any mention of Christ's sacrifice or even the people's sacrifice of praise and thanksgiving. Although Zwingli did not completely reject the eucharistic presence of Christ, his view reduced to very little importance this traditional theological theme. He rejected Luther's belief in the ubiquity of Christ and claimed that Christ's humanity was strictly localized in heaven; yet he did admit that in Christ's divine nature, which was spiritual, he could be present everywhere. Therefore, he acknowledged that Christ was figuratively represented in the service of the Lord's Supper.

Zwingli's sacramental doctrines, especially concerning the Lord's Supper, precipitated severe dissension and animosity between the Swiss Reformed Church and the Lutheran churches of Europe. Yet of more significance for our subject, Zwingli's views of the Lord's Supper logically led to his rejection of the Eucharist as the primary and normal service of public worship. That which had been the Sunday service and chief means of Christian worship since New Testament times was cast aside by Zwingli and his followers in favor of what became known as the Sunday Preaching Service. Zwingli ordered the Holy Communion to be celebrated only four times a year, and then as an addition to the regular Preaching Service. Therefore, the fact that quarterly Communion became standard practice not only in the Reformed churches of Europe and America but also in most Lutheran, Anglican, and Free churches until recent times is the legacy of the Zurich reformer in the history of Christian worship.

Zwingli's Preaching Service was conducted exclusively by the minister from the pulpit, which replaced the altar as the center of the Church's worship. The congregation had no part in the service; the assistant minister even offered the "Amen" at the end of the prayers on behalf of the congregation. Unlike Luther, Zwingli strongly opposed church music, and there was none in his service. Later most Reformed churches restored some music to the Sunday service, but never with the evangelical fervor of the Lutheran churches.

The order and content of the Preaching Service varied somewhat among the Reformed churches, but generally the service began with the minister's offering an opening prayer followed by the Lord's Prayer, which he recited himself. Then came the reading of a Scripture lesson, after which he preached a sermon on the passage read. After the sermon the minister in some order or another usually recited again the Lord's Prayer followed by the Decalogue, the Apostles' Creed, and a general confession with an assurance of pardon. It is noteworthy that even the general confession was recited by the minister alone. It can be recognized that the medieval Prone service was a major source for the Reformed Preaching Service.

Zwingli also produced two revisions of the medieval Mass: first a Latin version in 1523 and then a German vernacular service in 1525. The German service influenced later orders for the service of the Lord's Supper in the Reformed churches. Generally, Zwingli took the same approach as Luther in liturgical revision by deleting from the old service what he did not like or what did not agree with his doctrines. In his Latin service of 1523, Zwingli did evidence some potential for creativity in liturgy. Instead of simply reducing the Prayer of Consecration to Jesus' words of institution, Zwingli sought to rewrite it in the form of four separate prayers. In these prayers he retained some of the ancient eucharistic themes such as thanksgiving for creation and redemption and an idea of *anamnesis*. However, in his German service of 1525 all this was swept away; as with Luther, the Prayer of Consecration consisted only of the words of institution, and Communion immediately followed the recital of these words.

The Zurich reformer carried to a far greater extreme than Luther the pedagogical, or instructive, approach to Christian worship. In the regular Sunday Preaching Service, the congregation was to listen to, and be edified or instructed by, the minister. Zwingli's Communion Service also had a strongly didactic tone. The congregation participated only in reciting antiphonally the Gloria in Excelsis (which came between the Epistle and Gospel), receiving the Communion, and reciting antiphonally Psalm 113 after Communion. The Zurich service had the same fixed Collect, Epistle, and Gospel for every celebration of the Lord's Supper. But variety was hardly necessary when the service took place only four times a year, and then as an appendage to the Preaching Service. The Collect, like all Zwingli's prayers, was strongly didactic in tone for it sought to acquaint the worshiper with the meaning of the service. The Epistle was always Paul's account of the Last Supper in I Corinthians, Chapter 11, and the Gospel was always from the sixth chapter of John. The Communion proper began with an exhortation explaining the Reformed meaning of the Communion, followed by a "fencing of the table" in which the congregation was strongly warned not to come to receive Communion unworthily. After the minister alone recited the Lord's Prayer, he offered another prayer which explained God's mercy through the work of Christ, and man's unworthiness. Then followed the words of institution and the Communion, which was received in a seated position. Zwingli initiated sitting for Communion, a practice later widely adopted in Protestantism.

As one views Zwingli's lack of interest in sacraments, his deprecation of sacramental and especially eucharistic theology, his making the Preaching Service the norm for Sunday worship with the Communion appended to it four times a year, his almost complete prohibition of lay involvement in the services, and his idea that the function of worship was to teach the worshiper the content and meaning of the new religion, one can readily see the vast influence Zwingli had on the development of Protestant worship. For all of these elements became strongly embedded in the worship of most Protestant churches.

CALVIN OF GENEVA

John Calvin made the most significant contributions to Protestant theology, church government, and ecclesiastical discipline of all the sixteenth-century reformers. As a theologian he was more systematic and influential than either Luther or Zwingli. Concerning worship, however, Calvin presents a puzzling paradox. Although he had a strong doctrine of sacraments, especially the Eucharist, Calvin, the creative theologian, showed little interest in liturgy. Usually he adopted, or acceded to, the forms of service he found in the places where he went to minister.

In contrast to Zwingli, for example, Calvin believed the sacraments were a means of God's grace. He did not, however, care for the objective realism and doctrine of sacraments taught both by traditional Christianity and by Luther. In the sacrament of the Lord's Supper, Calvin also reacted against Zwingli by holding a high doctrine, but at the same time he refused to follow Luther's more traditional beliefs. For Calvin the Eucharist involved a spiritual feeding in which the believer received the virtue or power of Christ's passion. Moreover, through the interaction of the Spirit of God, working through the material elements, with the Christian's personal faith, the believer participated really but spiritually in the life of the Risen Lord Christ. In other words, Calvin maintained a real but spiritual eucharistic presence of Christ, placing him on something of a middle ground between Zwingli and Luther. He cared neither for Luther's localized objective presence of the Lord in the elements nor for Zwingli's almost complete denial of Christ's presence. Therefore, he carefully strove to construct a doctrine of spiritual presence.

Calvin's eucharistic doctrine becomes stronger when one considers that throughout his life he desired the Lord's

Supper to be the primary form of Christian worship. For
Calvin the Sunday service should be the Eucharist, the chief
service of public worship from the beginning of Christendom. In actual practice, however, the Geneva reformer
never realized his personal conviction about the Eucharist,
for historical circumstances prevented acceptance of his
eucharistic ideas.

When in 1536 Calvin first became a preacher and theological professor in Geneva, a Protestant Reformed church
had already been founded by William Farel, an ardent
disciple of Zwingli. The Sunday service was a Zwinglian
Preaching Service; the Communion was celebrated infrequently as an appendage to the Preaching Service. Although
Calvin did not seek to change the liturgical rite, he did seek
in 1537 to allow a weekly celebration of the Eucharist. In
this he was defeated by Farel and the political government
of Geneva, which in typical sixteenth-century fashion had
to approve all changes in religion. A political upheaval in
Geneva in 1538 forced Calvin to leave the city and become
the first minister of a newly formed French Protestant congregation in the free city of Strasbourg. Calvin was a Frenchman by birth and education. In Strasbourg he revealed his
lack of interest in the matter of liturgical worship. Since he
was the first minister of a new congregation, he had the
opportunity to reform the old service or to create and experiment with new forms of worship. Yet all he did was to
accept, and to translate into French, the service of the German Protestant church in Strasbourg.

This German church in Strasbourg was a unique com-
bination of Lutheranism and Zwinglianism. It had begun as
a Lutheran church in the 1520's, but under the leadership of
its chief minister, Martin Bucer, it had become more Zwinglian in the thirties. Bucer himself had been a disciple of
Luther who later accepted some of Zwingli's doctrinal and
liturgical ideas. He then sought to mediate between the two

forms of Protestantism by combining the two in a single church in Strasbourg.

Following the Lutheran pattern, the context of the Sunday service in the German church was the Eucharist, but the full Communion was celebrated only monthly. Calvin readily adopted both the form of the service and the full monthly Communion. When in 1541 another political and ecclesiastical upheaval in Geneva resulted in many of Calvin's supporters gaining political power, Calvin was called back to the Swiss city as its chief minister. There he remained until his death in 1564.

Once back in Geneva, Calvin sought to introduce the Strasbourg service with a weekly Communion, but the Zwinglian influence still remained too strong, and he had to compromise. The context of the Sunday service would be the Strasbourg Eucharist, but the full Communion would be allowed only once a month. On the non-communion Sundays, all the parts of the service pertaining to the Communion were deleted. The result was in a sense a rather full Preaching Service or a somewhat extended Ante-Communion. Calvin also had to delete some parts of the Strasbourg service which were repugnant to the Geneva ecclesiastical and political leaders. For example, the Strasbourg absolution after the General Confession and the singing of the Decalogue with a Kyrie Eleison response to each commandment were too richly liturgical for the Swiss Protestants and were deleted. In fact, the only music allowed in the Geneva service was the singing of a Psalm in meter.

From the Zwinglian disciple Farel, and from his Strasbourg experience, Calvin absorbed the growing Protestant emphasis upon corporate worship as pedagogical and congregational participation as essentially unimportant. His Geneva service was heavily didactic: the minister recited the Lord's Prayer in a long interpretative paraphrase; and when the full Communion was celebrated, the minister read a long exhortation on the meaning of the Communion after the words of institution and before the reception of the sacrament. The congregation's participation in the service was limited to singing the metrical Psalm; the other parts of the worship were done by the minister.

THE FREE CHURCHES OF EUROPE

Although the Lutheran and Reformed churches were not as richly liturgical as Western Christianity had been in the early and medieval periods, nevertheless these new Protestant bodies were liturgical churches. A liturgical church has two chief characteristics: first, the order of all the services has a set form. (Most of the reformers provided forms for Baptism, Marriage, and Burial of the Dead in addition to the Sunday Preaching or Communion services.) In a liturgical church the content of the prayers is also fixed, but variations or alternatives are frequently provided. Secondly, in a liturgical church this set form and content are established by a highly authoritative person or governing body as the standard of worship to be used in all the churches under the jurisdiction of that person or government.

In sixteenth-century Protestantism the authority usually was the political government. At that time Church and state, religion and politics, had not been divided; each was held to be concerned with, and responsible for, the other. Therefore, whether it was the diet (or parliament) of a German duchy, the council of a Swiss city, the king of Sweden, or the Crown and Parliament of England, the state decided the official religion including its doctrine and liturgy. Usually the ecclesiastical leaders such as Luther in Wittenberg, Bucer in Strasbourg, and Calvin in Geneva would submit their proposals for the doctrine, discipline, and worship of the Church for government approval. Occasionally, as with Calvin in Geneva, the ecclesiastical leaders were forced to amend or compromise their views in order to gain acceptance for the rest of their program.

Although these major Protestant churches in the sixteenth century were liturgical, there arose at that time on the Continent, and especially in Scotland and England, small sects or churches which took a completely nonliturgical approach to Christian worship. Although these churches gave themselves various names, on the Continent they were usually referred to as Anabaptists and in England and Scotland were labeled Independents, Separatists, and Puritans. (As will be seen later, the English Puritans initially opposed only the Anglican Prayer Book, but eventually, under the influence of the Independents, most Puritans adopted a free-worship approach to liturgy.)

The three main characteristics of free-worship churches were that the local congregation and minister decided the worship for the local church; that a fixed order of service was unnecessary; and especially that fixed, or set, prayers were wrong and must be replaced with extemporary prayer. Since these churches held the literal word of Scripture as their only authority and guide in all matters, the preaching of lengthy sermons upon biblical passages was the primary and almost sole feature of their services. Customarily, the only other element in the service was an extemporary prayer by the preacher before and after the lesson and sermon. Needless to say, of all the emerging Protestant churches, the Free churches carried to the greatest extreme the ideas that the congregation should not participate in the service and that the service's chief purpose was to instruct or edify.

The Free churches maintained Baptism and the Lord's Supper, but these services were done infrequently using the simplest rites. The Lord's Supper was celebrated no more than four times a year and in many churches only once a year. Usually its only form was the recital of Jesus' words of

institution and the distribution of the bread and the cup to
the seated congregation after the sermon. At times the bread
and cup were distributed with no words or form used. Many
of the Free churches discarded the services of Marriage and
Burial of the Dead as civil functions having no warrant in
Scripture. Also discarded as unwarranted by Scripture were
the Church Year and any sign of vestments, ceremonies, and
ecclesiastical ornaments.

During the sixteenth and early seventeenth centuries, the
free-worship churches in Europe generally lacked political
support; therefore, they were frequently persecuted, not
only by Roman Catholics but by Lutherans in Germany,
Calvinists in Switzerland and Scotland, and Anglicans in
England. Such persecution forced them either to conform
bitterly to the established Church while maintaining their
own secret associations and awaiting a more tolerant Europe,
or to flee to the New World when America began to be
colonized in the seventeenth century. The fact that many
of the first colonists in the New World were free-worship
churchmen fleeing from religious persecution in England has
been the most significant factor in the development of American Protestant worship. To this day the majority of American
Protestant denominations are free-worship churches. For example, although the highest legislative bodies of the largest
branches of Methodism and Presbyterianism in America have
in recent years authorized revised liturgical service books,
it remains the prerogative of the local minister and congregation as to whether the services in these liturgical books
will be used. Often they are not. Such is the pattern in many
American Protestant churches today, and this is the legacy
of the free-worship churches of the sixteenth century.

The Roman Church and the Counter Reformation

Traditional Western Latin Christendom, centered
in the Church of Rome and the papacy, did not stand idly

by as its doctrine and structure were attacked and rent asunder by the Protestant reformers. Through the founding of some new religious orders, notably the Society of Jesus (Jesuits), through the efforts of a succession of strong popes beginning in the 1530's, and especially through the work of the Council of Trent, which met in twenty-five sessions from 1545 to 1563, the Roman Catholic Church valiantly resisted the attempts to establish Protestantism throughout western Europe. The result was a partial victory for all. Spain, Italy, Ireland, and France remained predominantly Roman Catholic countries, whereas Scandinavia, England, Scotland, and parts of Germany, Switzerland, and the Low Countries accepted Protestantism in one form or other.

Two aspects characterized the Roman Church's Counter Reformation in the sixteenth century: defense and conservatism. What the medieval Church had established as the doctrine, discipline, worship, and structure of the Church, sixteenth-century Roman Catholicism sought to defend and conserve as absolute truth. In the matter of worship this meant that the Council of Trent restated the medieval formulations of sacramental grace, Transubstantiation, eucharistic sacrifice, and the doctrine of merit. Thus, that which the reformers had sought to reform or had discarded was made even more absolute by the decrees of Trent.

Concerning worship, Trent was too busy with theological and doctrinal matters to deal with the services of the Church. Occasionally during the long period of the council, opinions were voiced about attending to liturgical needs, but with the exception of some statements about too many votive masses, too many saints' days, the need for more frequent Communion, and the desire for a uniform and standard Roman Catholic missal, no definitive decrees were made about the Church's worship.

Ultimately the council left liturgical matters for the papacy to deal with, and in July, 1570, Pope Pius V, following the work of a papal liturgical commission, promulgated a uniform missal for the Roman Catholic Church. In many ways this was a revolutionary step in the history of Western Christian worship, for no pope had ever sought to make a uniform rite for Catholic Christendom. Theoretically in the Middle Ages any religious or monastic order or any diocese or cathedral could use whatever services it pleased. As we have noted, though, by the later Middle Ages all the churches and orders of Latin Christendom had for many reasons adopted the services of the Church of Rome. Except for a rare difference in liturgical content, the only variations in Western services were in matters of ceremonial, private devotions of the priest in the services, and in the calendars of saints. Pius V's missal generally did away with even this slight diversity, except that any church which could prove it had used a variant custom for over two hundred years was allowed to retain it. For this reason some cathedrals such as those at Milan, Cologne, and Lyons were able to continue certain customs not included in the Roman rite.

In his decree of 1570, Pius V did eliminate some saints' days from the Roman calendar, and he placed some minor restrictions on the use of votive masses. Otherwise the medieval rite became the absolute norm for Roman Catholic worship. Pope Sixtus V, in 1588, carried Pius's idea even further by creating a Congregation of Rites whose chief purpose was to see that the Church's rites were uniformly practiced everywhere. Although two minor revisions were made in the Roman missal in the seventeenth century, no real revision or renewal of official Roman Catholic worship took place until the twentieth century. Some reform of the Roman services was initiated in 1920; this work was accelerated in the 1940's and 1950's by Pope Pius XII and has culminated, for the moment at least, in the dramatic changes in Roman liturgy wrought by the recent Vatican Council and Pope Paul VI.

Most Roman Catholic liturgical scholars today readily deplore the state of liturgy and worship in the Roman Church from the latter part of the sixteenth century until recent times. The Counter Reformation's emphasis on a tight uniformity of liturgical rites which were based on the medieval services only perpetuated the worst errors of the medieval period. In fact, the medieval problems were accentuated in the seventeenth and eighteenth centuries. The Sunday service of the Mass became even more the priest's act, and the people were further removed from participation in the Church's worship. Yet in order to keep the congregation occupied and edified, additional efforts were made to provide personal devotions and especially to enhance the color, music, and ceremonial of the services. Ornate and richly colorful vestments, paintings, and statues, as well as more elaborate ceremonies, were multiplied to give the congregation something to look at during the service. And for the ear, there were developed incredibly elaborate musical pieces. Sometimes choirs sang these pieces throughout the Mass, even though the music bore little relation to the service being conducted by the priest at the altar. In other words, the priest did one thing, the choir another, while the people gazed and listened. All of the pomp and ornamentation of the Baroque period in Western culture were employed to make the Sunday service "a good show."

In addition to the elaboration of color, ceremony, and ornate music, Roman worship from the seventeenth through the nineteenth century was characterized by a constant emphasis on doctrines, especially those of eucharistic presence and sacrifice. Since the Protestants continued to inveigh against these doctrines, Roman Catholics continued to exalt them. A result of the post-Reformation emphasis on Transubstantiation was the development and common use of extra-eucharistic services such as Adoration and Benediction of

the Blessed Sacrament. In these rites a Host previously consecrated at a Mass became the object of corporate and personal devotions by the congregation. A further result of this
doctrinal dogmatism involved the reception of Holy Communion. Although most laity received the sacrament only
once a year, it was administered outside of and separate from
the Mass itself, usually after an early Mass on Sunday. Thus,
the chief reason for, and natural climax of, the eucharistic
service—the Communion—was no longer part of the service
for the laity. In reality, however, this was simply a logical
conclusion of the early medieval emphasis on the Prayer of
Consecration as the climactic point of the service.

These extra-eucharistic services and practices provided,
of course, liturgical substitutes for the laity, for by the post-
Reformation period the Sunday Mass had become exceedingly remote from the congregation. In the three centuries
following the Reformation, occasional attempts were made
by priests and bishops, usually in France and Germany, to
involve the laity in the supposedly corporate worship of the
Church. These attempts were few and all ended in failure,
chiefly because the large majority of Roman Catholic clergy
and hierarchy preferred things as they were. Pope Alexander
VII typified the official attitude when in 1661 he forbade the
translation of the missal into French, and clearly asserted
that the Latin Mass was in no way to be given to the lay
people.

Many of these unfortunate liturgical developments
spawned by medieval and post-Reformation Catholicism
have been swept away by the twentieth-century liturgical
movement. Since the story of this liturgical renewal has been
told many times elsewhere, we need not recount it in detail
here. Although there were some vague stirrings during the
nineteenth century on the European continent, the Roman
liturgical movement really did not begin until the first decade of this century in Belgium under the leadership of Dom

Lambert Beauduin of the Abbey of Mont Cesar. He took the all-important first step for the recovery of corporate worship in the Roman Church by translating the missal into the vernacular. Actually this had only become possible in 1897 when Pope Leo XIII made a change in the Index, removing translations of the missal from this list of prohibited books. Now, although the actual Mass remained entirely in Latin, the laity at least had in their personal missals the service in their own language. This enabled the proponents of liturgical renewal to begin teaching the laity about the meaning of corporate worship; this in turn led to tentative experiments involving the congregation's participation in worship at least to the extent that the Roman Mass allowed. This teaching and experiment led finally to the vast reforms and recent changes made by the Vatican Council and Pope Paul VI in the early 1960's whereby most of the Mass and other services are in the vernacular, and the congregation has been called into real and fruitful participation in the worship of the Church.

PROTESTANT WORSHIP AFTER THE REFORMATION

The history of Protestant worship from the seventeenth through the nineteenth century is very similar to the history of Roman Catholic worship during the same period. It involved carrying to extreme but logical conclusions many liturgical ideas and practices which had begun to develop in the previous centuries. Even more ironic, perhaps, is that the pattern of worship in the Free churches (which were so severely persecuted by Lutheran, Reformed, and Anglican churches in the sixteenth century) became the way of worship for most of Protestantism in the post-Reformation period.

Throughout the Reformed churches and in many Lutheran churches (the Scandinavian Church excepted), free worship became the norm in the eighteenth and nineteenth centuries. The liturgical Preaching Service of Zwingli and Calvin became a free Preaching Service. The sermon was the basic feature, with the preacher offering lengthy prayers before and after it. The prayers were no longer from an authorized fixed liturgy but were extemporaneous. Many Lutherans even discarded Luther's liturgically truncated Mass for a similar free Preaching Service. The congregation participated only by singing metrical Psalms in the Reformed, and German hymns in the Lutheran, churches. These churches did continue to use prescribed liturgical forms for Baptism and the Lord's Supper, but these sacraments were rarely used. The Communion was celebrated no more than four times a year, and usually fewer. Moreover, in many Calvinist and Lutheran churches, the Lord's Supper became an appendage to the regular Sunday Preaching Service as it had already become in the Zwinglian and Free churches of the sixteenth century.

The greatest decline in Protestant worship occurred in its meaning and purpose, for by the eighteenth century the chief, even sole, purpose was to instruct and to edify the congregation. As in Free-church worship the lengthy sermon and the prayer were to teach the hearers in the pew the preacher's approach to doctrine and morality. Therefore, by the eighteenth century, as far as the congregation was concerned, whether it be Reformed, Lutheran, Free, or Roman Catholic, all idea was lost that the Sunday service involved *corporate* worship in which all the people of God, laity or clergy, offered their worship of praise and thanksgiving to God. The biblical and patristic understanding of Christian worship had succumbed to clericalism, moralism, and individualism.

The fact that so many Protestant liturgical churches of the Reformation became practically free-worship churches in the ensuing three centuries oddly enough cannot be directly attributed to the Anabaptists, Puritans, and Independents of the sixteenth century. Only in America, as we have noted, did the free-worship churches significantly influence the development of Protestant worship. In Europe two movements, pietism and rationalism, chiefly contributed to the rise of free worship in the Reformed and Lutheran churches. These movements were seventeenth- and eighteenth-century reactions to the strongly doctrinal and tightly organized Reformation churches.

Pietists, for example, whether Lutheran or Reformed, deprecated doctrinal definitions and confessions of faith, while they exalted personal spirituality and morality. The personal subjective experience, especially the conversion experience, became the chief factor in pietism. Concerning worship, the pietists placed personal prayer and Bible reading ahead of public worship. The Sunday service had its place only in that its central feature, the sermon, became a means of developing personal religion and a conversion experience. The rest of the service had to conform to the sermon. Therefore, extemporary prayer, which did not "quench the Spirit" as did liturgical prayer, and exceedingly subjective hymns, were all else that was needed. Pietists usually looked upon the Lord's Supper as a richly emotional personal experience to which one could not and should not be often exposed. Therefore, the Communion was rarely celebrated more than once a year.

Rationalism, which developed as a reaction against both pietism and the literal biblicism of the Reformation churches, exalted man's reason as the supreme way of knowing God. It deprecated revelation, especially biblical revelation. Like the reformers and the pietists, the rationalists found the pulpit to be the best means of publishing and inculcating their ideas. For them the sermon was the only really necessary element in public worship, for they disavowed liturgical forms and prayers as coming from an irrational past.

With pietism and rationalism rife in European Protestantism, and with Free churches based on a biblical literalism the predominant force in American Protestantism, corporate worship had by the nineteenth century reached its greatest decline. Yet it was also in that very nineteenth century that the recovery and renewal of Protestant corporate worship began. Before the end of the last century, almost all these churches—Lutheran, Reformed, and Free—had a few people within their membership, usually clergy, who saw the need for Protestant liturgical reform. Their accomplishments then were very few, but they laid the foundation for the renewal of public corporate worship throughout Protestantism in this century. Yet even in this century, Protestant liturgical renewal has often achieved only limited accomplishments. Its impact, however, upon the nature and direction of Protestant Christianity today does continue to increase.

Since there are so many Protestant churches throughout the world, in the past one hundred years there have naturally been many Protestant individuals and organizations which have influenced liturgical renewal. It is impossible, therefore, in this historical survey of Christian worship to give any kind of adequate treatment to these personalities and organizations. One source, however, which has continually influenced every individual and organization concerned with Protestant liturgical renewal is the Anglican Book of Common Prayer. In the past two centuries every official Protestant liturgical commission and every authorized Protestant service book has acknowledged its debt either to the Prayer Book of the Church of England or to that of the American Episcopal Church. We turn then to the English Reformation and the creation and development of the Anglican and American Prayer Books.

Chapter 7

Liturgy and the
English Reformation

THE MOMENTOUS Reformation legislation of 1532 to 1534 caused the Church *in* England to become the Church *of* England. Through this legislation, especially the Act of Supremacy of 1534, which made King Henry VIII the authoritative head of the English Church, the Christian Church in England became an independent, sovereign Church. No longer did the English Church have formal ties with, or owe obedience to, other churches or ecclesiastical figures such as the Church of Rome and the pope. The English Christian's highest ecclesiastical obedience now was to the English bishops, especially the Archbishop of Canterbury; but over the bishops and the whole Church was the state, personified by the Crown.

The legislation of the 1530's was, however, only a first

stage, albeit a key stage, in the formation of the Anglican Church. This first part of the English Reformation was much more political and jurisdictional than doctrinal and liturgical. In other words, the supreme authority and government of the English Church changed from pope and Curia to king with Parliament and bishops; but the doctrine, discipline, and worship of the Church changed hardly at all. The Latin services based on the rites of the Church of Rome, and the medieval formulations of Transubstantiation and eucharistic sacrifice, continued as official liturgy and doctrine throughout King Henry's reign until his death in 1547.

The political character of the first part of the English Reformation, together with its doctrinal and liturgical conservatism, is crucially important for understanding the history and meaning of Anglican worship to this day. When liturgical and theological change did take place in the English Reformation during the reigns of Edward VI (1547-1553) and Elizabeth I (1558-1603), the changes were not as revolutionary as those which had already taken place within the newly formed Protestant churches on the European continent. Many, though certainly not all, English reformers of the sixteenth century sought to preserve a sense of history within Anglicanism. Although dedicated to the principles of the Reformation, they wanted the English Church to be continuous with the Church of past ages, especially with the early Church, but even to some extent with the medieval Church.

Henry VIII's conservatism in doctrine and worship kept liturgical changes to a bare minimum during his reign. Toward the end of the 1530's, when Henry sought political and military alliances with some German Lutheran states, he allowed the English Bible to be placed in parish churches. The only real liturgical innovation of the reign was the publication and use in 1544 of an English litany. This was the first public service of worship in the English language. In

1544 England was at war with Scotland and France, and Henry wanted the people to pray for victory. When the English people showed little interest in the traditional Latin litanies for victory, the Archbishop of Canterbury, Thomas Cranmer, offered the king a litany in English which he had drawn up. The practical king liked Cranmer's work and authorized the litany to be used in all English churches. The first English litany was much like the one in the Anglican Prayer Books today, except that it included the ancient invocations of the Virgin Mary, the angels, and the saints, which have since been omitted.

Upon Henry's death in 1547, his ten-year-old son, Edward, ascended the English throne. Since the king was a boy, the king's council governed the nation throughout the short, less-than-seven-year reign of Edward VI. The membership of this council reflected the three types of religious persuasion present in England at the middle of the sixteenth century. First, there were the conservatives, who had liked Henry VIII's national Catholic Church with medieval doctrine and liturgy, but without submission to the pope and the Roman Church. Though this conservative position had few representatives on the council and little political influence, it had a fairly large following among the English people.

The second and largest group numerically and politically on the council were the moderate Protestant reformers, or, as they have been called, the Reformed Catholics, led by Archbishop Cranmer and Nicholas Ridley, the future Bishop of London. The moderates definitely sought to establish a reformed Church of England; yet they also insisted upon a reformed Church that would be continuous with the Church of the past. For example, they strongly opposed the medieval doctrines of the eucharistic sacrifice and the eucharistic presence of Christ, but they were not opposed to the ancient belief in sacrifice and presence. Rather, they sought new or revised formulations. The moderates also opposed excessive clericalism, yet they fully supported the traditional, threefold ministry and the episcopal government of the Church. These reformers had a strong aversion to many ceremonies in worship, but they did not seek to eliminate all color, music, and pageantry from the services.

The moderates were always in a majority on the council and probably had the largest following in the nation, but their political control lasted only from 1547 to 1550, when their leader, the Duke of Somerset, headed the council. After Somerset's fall from power in 1550 and until the death of King Edward in 1553, political control of council and nation was held by the council's third group, the extreme Protestants. Their leader and chief supporter was the somewhat unprincipled Earl of Warwick. He had no particular religious convictions, but he supported the extreme Protestants because he felt they could best aid him in the furtherance of his own political ambitions. Generally the extreme reformers followed the doctrinal teachings of the famous French reformer, John Calvin. However, in liturgy and eucharistic doctrine these reformers adhered to the more radical Swiss reformer, Huldreich Zwingli. The extreme English Protestants were numerically small both on the council and in the nation, but they were exceedingly zealous, worked very hard for their cause, and made themselves heard.

Soon after Edward came to the throne in 1547, liturgical experiment began in England. In that year the council decreed that the Epistle and Gospel at High Mass should be sung in the vernacular. This decree set in motion events which led to the first English Book of Common Prayer in 1549. (It is interesting that in 1954 Pope Pius XII made the first change in the Latin Mass of the Roman Catholic Church by allowing the Epistle and Gospel to be read in the vernacular. As in 1547, so in 1954 the allowance of Scripture lessons in the vernacular led to radical liturgical change, for in the

1960's the Second Vatican Council and Pope Paul VI have instituted vast changes in Roman Catholic worship.) During the first two years of Edward's reign, some larger churches, such as St. Paul's in London and the chapels at the universities, began unauthorized liturgical experiments by singing some of the choral parts of the Eucharist—Kyrie, Gloria in Excelsis, Sanctus, and Agnus Dei—in English.

The radical eucharistic views of the extreme Protestants stirred up so much controversy in England that in 1547 Parliament passed an act against the Revilers of the Sacrament. A provision of this act decreed that in England the Communion should be received in both kinds. However, no provision existed in the Latin Mass still in use for the congregation to receive from the chalice. The communion cup had been withheld from the laity in the Western Church for several hundred years. The medieval Church's extreme emphasis on the physical presence of Christ in the wine had caused the clergy concern that the wine would spill or that the laity would abuse its use. Besides this theologically based consideration for the withdrawal of the chalice from the laity during the Middle Ages, there was also a practical problem. Since most Christians received Communion only once a year, at Easter, the clergy came to believe that the Easter service would be expedited if the people received the bread only.

In 1547 the English Church faced the problem of how to accede to Parliament's decree ordering the chalice to be given to the laity when the Latin Mass did not provide for this. By March, 1548, Archbishop Cranmer had again solved the problem, but in his own way. Instead of making a simple change in the Latin service, he drew up an Order of Communion in English which was inserted into the Latin Mass after the priest received Communion. This Order of Communion consisted of two exhortations concerning one's preparation for receiving the Holy Communion, then the

Invitation, General Confession, Absolution, and Comfortable
Words as they still appear in the Anglican service today.
These were followed by the Prayer of Humble Access (We
do not presume to come to this thy Table, O merciful Lord,
etc.), the lay people's Communion in both kinds, and a blessing. The service then reverted to the Latin Mass.

Cranmer's Order of Communion marked the second time
in the 1540's that the archbishop had solved a liturgical problem with a new vernacular service. The English litany of
1544 and the Order of Communion of 1548 not only prepared
the way for the first English Prayer Book, but they demon-
strated the fine liturgical ability of Archbishop Cranmer.

THE FIRST ENGLISH PRAYER BOOK OF 1549

In recent years some Anglicans have been puzzled
or critical about Archbishop Cranmer's approach to worship.
He had been the chief architect of the first Book of Common
Prayer of 1549, a book highly favored by liturgical scholars
and most Anglicans. Yet three years later, in 1552, Cranmer
was also chiefly responsible for producing the second Book
of Common Prayer. This book turned out to be something of
a liturgical muddle. It is often called "a botched job." The
obvious question has been, How could the same man produce
both books?

The question is easily answered if two significant, but
sometimes neglected, factors are considered. First, the political side of the matter of English worship must be recognized. Politics became a determining factor at every turn
of the English Reformation. Second, one must consider the
liturgical sources Cranmer used and the major ecclesiastical
influences upon him as he was compiling each book. As a
matter of fact, the sources and influences were radically different in each case.

Cranmer began his liturgical projects in the 1530's, and

his chief source was the traditional service of the Church in England, known as the Sarum rite. During the later Middle Ages the English diocese of Sarum (or Salisbury) had developed services of the Church for an English setting. The basic order and content of all the services followed carefully the services of the Church of Rome, but the Sarum services differed somewhat from the Roman rites in use of ceremonial, in the colors used for vestments and altar, and in the wording of some minor prayers. Thus, the Sarum rite was basically the Roman rite with uniquely English changes and additions.

By the sixteenth century most English dioceses had adopted the Sarum-Roman rite for their worship. A few dioceses in the North of England used the York rite, and in the diocese of Hereford the Hereford rite was used. Like Sarum, however, these rites were basically the Roman services with changes in ceremonial, color, and a few minor prayers. The Sarum-Roman services occupied Cranmer's chief interest. They were the main source of the first English Prayer Book, and they remain to this day the foundation of Anglican worship.

Protestant and Roman Catholic liturgical works also influenced Cranmer's studies. A Roman Catholic liturgical scholar of the day whose ideas Cranmer studied carefully was the Spanish Cardinal Quignon. The archbishop was also quite familiar with Lutheran ideas and practices, and he adopted some elements from a Lutheran source into the first Prayer Book. This source is called Hermann's *Consultation*.

Hermann of Wied was Archbishop of Cologne in the 1540's when he decided to break from the Roman Church and become a Lutheran. Since he wanted the Cologne cathedral to become a Lutheran church, he persuaded some Lutheran theologians to aid him in drawing up a procedure, or consultation, for the establishment of a Lutheran church there. The liturgical parts of his *Consultation* were written

by three Lutheran theologians: Melanchthon, Bucer, and
Osiander. Cranmer was familiar not only with this work but
with the reply made by the clergy of the Cologne cathedral,
called the *Antididagma,* in which they refused to become
Lutherans or to adopt Lutheran worship, and offered their
reasons of refusal.

The English archbishop did not simply study sixteenth-
century sources, however. He read extensively about liturgy
and worship in the early church fathers. Also, unlike most
scholars of his day, Cranmer became familiar with the Eastern liturgies of Chrysostom and Basil. He may have been
familiar with the old Spanish, or Mozarabic, liturgy, at least
as it was celebrated in the cathedral of Toledo in the sixteenth century.

It is highly significant, then, that Cranmer's sources for
the first Prayer Book were chiefly ancient, traditional, Catholic sources with some influence from conservative Lutheranism. Although in theological doctrine Archbishop Cranmer
apparently liked some of the ideas of the more extreme Protestant reformers, liturgically he was conservative and traditional. He did, however, desire moderate and sensible reform
of the traditional services.

In addition to liturgical influences on Cranmer, England's
political atmosphere determined much of Cranmer's approach to liturgy and worship. As Archbishop of Canterbury
and a member of the king's council, he was a statesman as
well as a clergyman. In the late 1540's England was a divided
nation, chiefly because of religion. There were conservative
Catholics, moderates, and extreme reformers. The archbishop
wisely understood that England could not continue to grow
into a sovereign world power if the nation itself was divided.
Religious unity was necessary for England to have political
unity and a position of world power.

His astute knowledge of Church and state made him

realize that unity of doctrine or belief was impossible in England. Henry VIII had tried to achieve doctrinal unity in England and had failed; on the Continent the Protestants and Roman Catholics had failed to achieve doctrinal unity in some conversations during the early forties; and in fact the continental Protestants themselves were split over doctrinal matters.

Cranmer sought to achieve religious unity in England through worship. He went about creating a Book of Common Prayer which would be acceptable to as many Englishmen as possible, and which would comprehend as many of his countrymen as possible in a single, united Church of England. Cranmer believed that common worship should be the unity and heart of Anglicanism.

In order to achieve his goal, the archbishop sought to create a Prayer Book which would be doctrinally moderate, thereby appealing to most English Protestants, and which would be liturgically conservative, thereby winning English Catholics to his side. By the fall of 1548 he had drawn up such a Prayer Book, and the king's council created a commission of twelve scholars, including six bishops, to review Cranmer's work. This commission, which met at Windsor, made but few changes. Generally it rubber-stamped the archbishop's work. Actually Cranmer himself made some changes in the draft just before it was submitted to Parliament in December, 1548. His house guest in the fall of 1548 was John à Lasco, an extreme Protestant reformer from Poland who apparently succeeded in persuading Cranmer to make some alterations in a more Protestant direction. However, the Book of Common Prayer which was debated and passed by Parliament in December and January and given the royal assent on March 14, 1549, was basically the original doctrinally moderate and liturgically conservative draft of Cranmer's.

The book's doctrinal moderation between medieval Catholicism and extreme reformed Protestantism can be seen in its formulation of the eucharistic doctrines of sacrifice and the presence of Christ. Cranmer and his group strongly opposed the medieval doctrine of eucharistic sacrifice with its implication of a repetitive sacrifice of Christ and its resultant theology of merit. This opposition was reflected in Cranmer's toning down the importance of the offertory in the eucharistic service of the 1549 book. The ancient offertory concept of placing the bread and wine on the altar is mentioned once, while the offertory sentences and rubrical directions stress the people's giving of alms. Almsgiving overshadows the older offertory concept because medieval churchmen had associated offertory with a repetitive crucifixion of Christ. In the Prayer of Consecration, Cranmer carefully emphasized that the remembrance of Christ's one sacrifice in the historical past is all that is considered at the service. He further scored his point by eliminating the traditional theme of the offering of the bread and the cup from the Prayer of Consecration.

Cranmer did not eliminate the concept of eucharistic sacrifice from the service, however. Christ's sacrifice was emphasized, as was the people's sacrifice of praise and thanksgiving. Cranmer also included in the prayer an oblation of self—"We offer and present unto thee, O Lord, our selves, our souls and bodies, to be a reasonable, holy, and living sacrifice unto thee. . . ." In other words he sought to reform, not to discard, the ancient eucharistic doctrine of sacrifice.

As for the doctrine of Christ's presence in the Eucharist, the first Prayer Book was somewhat traditional and conservative. The Prayer of Consecration included Jesus' words of institution—"This is my body"—as well as the ancient *anamnesis* of his death and resurrection (Cranmer added the

Lord's ascension). The Prayer of Humble Access, which Cranmer largely composed himself, and the communion sentences strongly emphasized Christ's presence in the bread and wine.

In his theological writings on the meaning of the eucharistic service, Cranmer laid great emphasis upon the reception of the sacrament of Holy Communion. The benefit of Communion, one of the chief eucharistic themes of the New Testament and of the second-century Church but which later was neglected in favor of extreme views of eucharistic presence and sacrifice, was restored to prominence by the archbishop. In fact, this was the main emphasis in the Prayer Book service. In the rubrical directions at the end of the Communion Service, Cranmer exhorted the people to receive the sacrament, and declared that there should be no Eucharist at which only the priest received the Holy Communion.

Doctrinally the first Prayer Book was moderate, but liturgically it was conservative. The basic order and content of the services followed the traditional Sarum-Roman rite with some changes and additions from Cranmer's ancient and contemporary sources already mentioned. Cranmer translated into excellent English prose many of the Latin prayers of the Sarum services. Although today the Cranmerian language of the Prayer Book is out of date and often not easily understood, this prose nevertheless stands as among the best ever found in Christian liturgy and in English literature.

THE SERVICES OF THE FIRST PRAYER BOOK

The eucharistic order of service in 1549 was very traditional. For example, the service began with a full Psalm introit, a ninefold Kyrie, and the Gloria in Excelsis, just as the Western service had begun since the seventh century. The intercessions (the Prayer for the Whole State of Christ's Church) were included, as they had been since the fourth century, in the Prayer of Consecration. From the Eastern Church, Cranmer borrowed the idea of an *epiclesis*, or invocation of the Holy Spirit upon the bread and wine. His actual wording, based on Latin models, read: ". . . with thy holy spirit and word vouchsafe to bless and sanctify these thy gifts, and creatures of bread and wine, that they may be unto us the body and blood . . ." of Christ. Here is another indication of Cranmer's emphasis on the presence of Christ. The General Confession, Absolution, Comfortable Words, and Prayer of Humble Access, which were new additions to the liturgy from the Order of Communion of 1548, were placed just before the reception of Communion. After Communion the service ended fairly quickly, as in the early Church, with the Prayer of Thanksgiving and the blessing.

The order and content of the services of Baptism and Confirmation in the 1549 Prayer Book followed even more closely the traditional Sarum-Roman services. With rare exceptions the only changes, additions, or deletions in Baptism and Confirmation had to do with ceremonies usually associated with these services. Although the liturgical order of all services in the first Prayer Book was traditional and conservative, Cranmer did severely reduce or eliminate ceremonies in order to make the book acceptable to the reformed churchmen of England.

Eliminated as unnecessary in the baptismal service were a number of ancient ceremonies, such as breathing upon the candidate, the giving of salt, some but not all of the anointings, and the giving of a candle. Yet the first Prayer Book did keep some of the old ceremonies, such as the sign of the cross upon the candidate's forehead, the main anointing (known as the chrism), and the vesting of the newly baptized in a white garment. In Confirmation the archbishop dropped the anointing of the confirmand in favor of the laying on of hands by the bishop. This actually was a restoration of an early church practice that the medieval Church had eliminated from the service. In the Communion Service, Cranmer also removed some ceremonies such as the Gospel procession and the elevation of the Host in the Prayer of Consecration. At the consecration a rubrical direction which forbade an elevation was even added. Cranmer realized, however, that the matter of ceremonies—eliminating some, retaining others—would be a controversial issue between conservative and reformed elements in the Church. Thus, at the end of the 1549 book, Cranmer wrote a short essay entitled "Of Ceremonies, Why Some Be Abolished and Some Retained." In some notes at the end of this essay, Cranmer proposed what has become an Anglican principle concerning the use of personal ceremonies by individuals. He wrote, "They may be used or left as every mans devotion serveth without blame."

The most revolutionary element in the first Book of Common Prayer was the establishing of the services of Morning and Evening Prayer for all people in the Church. Prior to 1549 these services were used chiefly by friars, monks, and nuns as daily services in addition to the Holy Eucharist. As we shall see, Cranmer intended these services to be daily additions to the central service of the Holy Communion for all Christian laymen as well as monks and clergy.

The personal, private devotions of the Jews are probably the origin of the services of Morning and Evening Prayer. We know from the Old Testament that the Jews offered private prayers at various times in the day, perhaps three times as in the Book of Daniel or seven times as the Psalms indicate. The Gospels reveal that Jesus often went to a quiet place for prayer. Following the Jewish practice and Jesus' example, the early Christians continued regular private devotions. Sometimes, as the Book of Acts tells us, the first Christians gathered in one place for these devotions. This practice of daily prayer by each Christian either alone or in groups continued throughout the early centuries of the Church. Many sources speak of personal Christian devotions being offered upon rising, at noonday, and at bedtime.

Hippolytus' *The Apostolic Tradition* informs us that in Rome, at least, the clergy gathered each morning in the church building for their private prayers. Often the laity would gather with them for these devotions. In the third and fourth centuries during the weeks before Easter, bishops (or presbyters appointed by the bishops) gave daily instruction to adults seeking Baptism and Confirmation. Lessons from Scripture were read and prayers offered at these instructions. It is significant, however, that neither the daily personal prayers of Christians nor the lessons and prayers appended to baptismal instruction developed a universal shape or form such as the Eucharist had achieved by the third century.

The saying of prayers in common or appending prayers to catechumen instruction remained as a form of nonliturgical worship for almost three centuries until the development of Christian monasticism. After a quiet beginning toward the end of the third century, monasticism became both popular and powerful within Christianity from the fourth century until the Reformation. Early in the fourth century the monks began to create liturgical services out of these nonliturgical private devotions. The services consisted of Scripture lessons, Psalms, and a few intercessory prayers. By the end of the fourth century the monks of the Eastern Church had developed Lauds and Vespers, which later formed two of eight monastic services. The monastic rule written in the beginning of the sixth century by the founder of Western monasticism, St. Benedict, indicates that all eight services had been established as the daily worship for monks. Nocturns came before dawn, Lauds at dawn, Prime, Terce, Sext, and None at the first, third, sixth, and ninth hours of the day, Vespers at sundown, and Compline at bedtime.

The chief purpose of these daily services of Psalms, lessons, and prayers was the corporate offering of praise and thanksgiving. The monastic community offered in common at eight different times in each day its private devotions. By the High Middle Ages even the secular clergy were obliged to read these daily services either together or privately. Two monastic services, Lauds and Vespers, even became somewhat popular with the laity during the Middle Ages; this was especially true in England, where some of the cathedrals and many of the parish churches were served by monks rather than by secular clergy. Although a large number of lay persons in pre-Reformation England attended Lauds and Vespers on Sundays and holy days, the laity were not required to attend them. Neither they nor the clergy looked upon these services as a substitute for the regular and central worship of the Church in the Eucharist. In fact, the Eucharist came after Lauds in England. In the so-called age of faith, people did not mind going to church early on Sunday and attending two services; nor at a time when there was little else to do, did they mind returning to church for Vespers at sundown. In fact they enjoyed it.

Archbishop Cranmer relied heavily on English interest when he formulated the services of Morning and Evening Prayer, which in the first Prayer Book were called Matins and Evensong. Cranmer's purpose in creating these services was to change them from monastic and clerical services into daily services for the laity. Like Luther and Calvin, Archbishop Cranmer firmly believed in the priesthood of all believers. No essential difference existed between clergy or monks and laity; ordination or religious life did not of themselves make people more holy or sanctified than ordinary laity. With regard to worship, Cranmer reasoned that since the clergy and monks came together daily for Psalms, lessons, and prayers, so the laity, who were equal to them, should do also. Then, too, since monasticism had been abolished in England in the late 1530's, the archbishop felt that a void had been created in the daily worship of Englishmen which could be filled by having all the people of God worship together daily in the parish church.

The eight somewhat complicated monastic services were not suited to lay worship, so Cranmer sought to reduce them in number and format. Previous efforts by Martin Luther and Cardinal Quignon to simplify the monastic services aided Cranmer in creating a morning and an evening service for the first English Prayer Book. Matins, later called Morning Prayer, was based on the monastic services of Nocturns, Lauds, and Prime. Evensong, later called Evening Prayer, was based largely on monastic Vespers with the addition of a few items from Compline. The services of Morning and Evening Prayer today are quite similar to Cranmer's Matins and Evensong in the first Prayer Book. The only major difference is that the Opening Sentences, General Confession, and Absolution were absent from the 1549 book. The services began, as had been traditional, with the versicles and responses.

Cranmer's ideal, then, called for the clergy and laity to gather in the parish church daily for Matins and Evensong. The Eucharist—called the Mass in sixteenth-century England, even in the first Prayer Book—would continue to be the main Sunday service, but Matins would precede the Communion. On Sunday evening, as before, all would return to the church for Evensong. Cranmer's pattern of worship was never actualized. The laity hardly comprehended the doctrine of the priesthood of all believers in the sixteenth century, for the pre-Reformation Church had so distinguished clergy from laity that the latter never really understood their equality with the clergy. In the matter of worship the laity had no tradition, inclination, or perhaps time, to worship twice daily in the parish church. Although Cranmer's efforts to produce a *daily* morning and evening service for all Christians failed, his Matins and Evensong became and have continued to be the daily services for Anglican clergy even to this day. The parish clergy of the Church of England are required by canon law to read in the church the daily services of Morning and Evening Prayer.

The pattern of Sunday worship envisioned by Cranmer also failed in Reformation England. Like Luther and Calvin, he believed that the Eucharist should continue to be the chief worship of Christians on Sunday. All the reformers, however, English and continental, insisted that every person in the congregation should receive the Holy Communion at each celebration of the Lord's Supper. But again there was no tradition for this. In fact, for centuries many laymen had received the sacrament only once a year. That was the norm, and no matter how much the reformers inveighed against it, the people refused to come forward and receive the Holy Communion.

The moderate reformers' disappointment over the laity's refusal to receive the sacrament frequently, together with the radical Protestants' disdain for the eucharistic service, caused a change in Cranmer's pattern of Sunday worship by the early 1550's. Sunday morning worship came to begin with Matins (Morning Prayer) followed by the Ante-Communion, the first part of the Eucharist up to the offertory. Later in the same decade the Litany was added to the order of service, so that for over three hundred years, from about 1560 until the end of the nineteenth century, the order for Anglican Sunday worship consisted of Morning Prayer, the Litany, and Ante-Communion with sermon. The full Communion Service was celebrated in some places once a month, but usually it was celebrated four times a year, on Christmas, Easter, Whitsunday, and in the autumn. Thus, the Eucharist,

which was based on Jesus' Last Supper and which had been
the chief Sunday service throughout Christendom since New
Testament times, was replaced by a pattern and order of
service which, although it was proclaimed to be reformed
and Protestant, was really medieval and monastic.

THE FAILURE OF THE FIRST PRAYER BOOK

Many Anglicans in the past century looked upon
the first English Prayer Book of 1549 as the classic one in
Anglican worship. Throughout the Anglican Communion
most Prayer Book revisions in this century have used the
1549 book as a model and have reincorporated many features
of that book into the services of the Church. In the midst of
this acclaim it is sometimes startling to realize that in its own
day the 1549 Prayer Book was a complete failure. The book
failed because the very idea of a uniform Prayer Book for
all was too radical in the sixteenth century. It failed also because Cranmer's attempts at moderation, compromise, and
comprehension were terribly revolutionary in an age when
these things were not the order of the day.

The mighty medieval Church never had an authoritative,
prescribed liturgy. The English had their Sarum version of
the Roman rite, the French had their Gallican versions, and
each monastic order had its version of the Roman services.
No pope ever ordered a common, uniform worship for the
Roman Catholic Church until Pius V in 1570. This was over
twenty years after the first English Prayer Book. No Protestant reformer was ever able to find wide acceptance for a
particular liturgy. Before Cranmer's first Book of Common
Prayer, the services of the Church were scattered among various liturgical books. These books were the property of the
clergy; they were almost unknown to the laity. The daily
monastic services were printed in a book called the breviary;
the eucharistic service was in the missal; the services of

Baptism, Marriage, and Burial of the Dead were in the priest's manual; and Confirmation and Ordination were in the bishop's pontifical. When Cranmer put all these services into one comprehensive Book of Common Prayer, the clergy and especially the laity had something they never had before. What could be more revolutionary?

Cranmer's attempt at moderation was also out of step with the sixteenth-century temper. A Prayer Book which was moderate theologically and conservative liturgically was anathema to some of the moderate, and all of the extreme, English reformers. The traditional structure of the services, the failure to excise all ideas of sacrifice and eucharistic presence, the keeping of vestments and some ceremonies, elicited strong dissent from the English Protestants, still a minority in England. Few of the more radical of the reforming clergy used the book as it had been published. They circumvented it, changed it, used it as they pleased.

The conservative churchmen also disliked the book because medieval formulations of eucharistic presence and sacrifice had been toned down or weakened, and many traditional ceremonies had been deleted. Conservative hostility was even more noticeable than that of the reformers. Edmund Bonner, Bishop of London, refused to use it and preached against it. He was sent to prison. In England's west, in Devon and Cornwall, the nobility and peasants opened an armed rebellion against the Crown. Although economic and political grievances were involved in the rebellion, religious dissatisfaction was offered as the chief cause of the rising. The rebels called upon the government to throw out the Prayer Book and restore the Latin rite. They also demanded the official acceptance and restoration of more conservative doctrines and liturgical ceremonies.

By the end of the summer of 1549, the only authoritative figures still supporting the Prayer Book were Cranmer and

Somerset, the Lord Protector. By late fall, however, Somerset had fallen from power. Although the religious rebellion in the west country, as well as two other rebellions which were strongly economic and political in cause, had been put down, Somerset could not survive the poor results of his economic policies and the political intriguing of his rival, the Earl of Warwick. By the beginning of 1550, Warwick had won control of the boy-king and the council and had gained the position of Lord Protector. Warwick is not a favorable figure in English history because most of his efforts were spent trying to establish a new dynasty for himself and his family.

One of the English government's severest problems at the time was lack of money. Therefore Warwick sought out all means to build up the treasury, thereby enhancing his own power. One of the chief sources of revenue coveted by the new Lord Protector was the wealth of the Church. As elsewhere in Western Christendom throughout the Middle Ages, the Church in England had gained great wealth in land, buildings, and endowment. Henry VIII began on a small scale to plunder the Church's wealth for the sake of the state's treasury. Warwick continued the enterprise on a larger scale. To his great delight he found a segment of the English Church willing to give up church funds to the state. The radical Protestants were quite willing to let the state have ecclesiastical endowments if the state would support more extreme Protestantism in England. The radical English Protestants were sincerely religious in making this political-ecclesiastical deal. They believed that their "new gospel" was the true religion; therefore, any means should be used to bring the truth to England. Also they believed that the Church's vast wealth inhibited the acceptance of their new gospel.

Warwick's support of the radical Protestants caused a shift in ecclesiastical power in England. The conservative churchmen, clerical or lay, went abroad, into hiding or retirement at home, or to prison. Almost all the conservative bishops were imprisoned. The moderate reformers such as Cranmer and Ridley also found their influence and power eclipsed. The more extreme reformers such as John Hooper, Bishop of Gloucester, Miles Coverdale, Bishop of Exeter, John Ponet, Bishop of Winchester, and John Knox, later an establisher of the Presbyterian Church of Scotland, became the leading ecclesiastical advisers to the protector and the king.

These changes in the Church-state structure in 1550-1551 quickly affected the worship of the Church. Goaded on by Hooper, who severely disliked the 1549 book, Warwick, with the king's assistance, demanded that the bishops produce a new Book of Common Prayer. Although many of the bishops had misgivings about the first book, few wanted to embark so soon on a new liturgy. Warwick so threatened the bishops, however, that by 1552 they were ready to revise the book. Moreover, as had happened on two occasions before, Cranmer was already at work on a draft to revise the worship of the Church.

The Second Book of Common Prayer

Cranmer's sources for the second Book of Common Prayer differed greatly from those which influenced the first Prayer Book. The 1549 book had been based chiefly upon the Sarum-Latin rite as well as ancient Greek and other Western rites and some conservative Lutheran ideas. The second book, of 1552, was influenced by moderate, but more especially by extreme, Protestant reformers.

The archbishop was greatly disillusioned because of the severe criticism of the first book by some continental reformers whom he highly respected. Cranmer had brought Martin Bucer to England in the late forties and gained for him a professorship at Cambridge. After reading the first

Prayer Book, Bucer wrote a very detailed criticism of the liturgical structure, contents, theology, and ceremonies of each service. Another less detailed but equally critical appraisal of the 1549 book was made by Pietro Vermigli (known in England as Peter Martyr). Peter Martyr was an Italian reformer of the Zwinglian school whom Cranmer had invited to England and had set up as a professor at Oxford. In addition to the continental reformers' strident criticism of the first book, Cranmer constantly faced barbs against the book by Hooper, Coverdale, Ponet, and other radical English reformers.

Negative criticism was not the archbishop's only source for the second book. He also had actual liturgical texts, but they, too, came from the radical side. Many continental refugees came to England in the late forties and early fifties because of the religious wars and persecutions on the Continent. Usually these refugees organized their own churches in and around London. The pastor of the Flemish Church in London at the time was Valerand Poullain, who earlier had succeeded John Calvin as pastor of the church in Strasbourg. In 1551 Poullain provided Cranmer with a Latin version of the worship used by his refugee congregation, a version based on Calvin's Strasbourg liturgy. In the same year the radical Polish reformer John à Lasco became pastor of a foreign church in London. He, too, gave Cranmer a copy of his Zwinglian type of service.

Since Cranmer's liturgical influences in the early fifties were so markedly reformed in contrast to the traditional sources he had consulted in the forties, it was hardly surprising that when a new Act of Uniformity containing a new Book of Common Prayer was passed by Parliament in the spring of 1552, this Prayer Book was quite reformed in character. That the 1552 book was such a strongly reformed liturgy is not to be lamented in itself, even though the book was a result of political-ecclesiastical expediency. The tragedy of the 1552 book was its liturgical ineptness, for it lacked sound principles in the order and content of the services. Fragmentation and confusion abounded.

More lamentable, no doubt, is the fact that until the twentieth century throughout the Anglican Communion, and to this day in the Church of England and in the American Episcopal Church, the poorly constructed 1552 Prayer Book has been the chief basis for worship. Today the Prayer Book of the Church of England is almost identical with the 1552 book. Although the Episcopal Church has revised her book somewhat in this century, the outline or order of the services is still very similar to the 1552 Book of Common Prayer. We shall see in a later chapter how this came to pass.

The fragmentation and confusion in the 1552 book occurred because Cranmer sought both to maintain his own principles and to satisfy the criticisms and demands of others. The archbishop still believed that worship as set forth in a Book of Common Prayer should be the principle of unity for the Anglican Church. He further continued to believe that in order to comprehend as many Englishmen as possible the book should be liturgically conservative and doctrinally moderate. Yet he was fully cognizant of the criticisms and demands of the radical reformers for more reformation in the Church of England. Cranmer's plight, the result of which in many ways still governs Anglican worship, was his attempt to satisfy everybody's demands including his own.

The radical reformers' chief complaints about the 1549 book centered in the Communion Service. In this service, Cranmer diligently sought to accede to their demands without negating all his own ideas. The first book called for the presiding minister at the Eucharist to wear the traditional alb and chasuble. Although the reformers found all vestments distasteful, Cranmer retained vestments; but in place of the ancient alb and chasuble, he substituted the surplice as the clergyman's vestment for the services in the parish church. The reformers disliked music, so the archbishop had to delete the ancient musical beginning, which had consisted of introit, Kyrie, and Gloria in Excelsis. However, Cranmer was so fond of the Gloria, and so aware of its long and good tradition in the Christian Eucharist, that he refused to delete it altogether. Instead, he placed the Gloria at the end of the service as a hymn of thanksgiving before the blessing. Although this displacement unfortunately lengthened the end of the service, which already had a prayer of thanksgiving after Communion, nevertheless it is to Cranmer's credit that this ancient Christian hymn was retained at all. The reformers also emphasized penitence in their services and criticized the first book for not stressing it enough. Thus, in the 1552 book Cranmer added the Decalogue at the beginning of the service to replace the deleted musical elements. The addition of the Ten Commandments was not an original idea with Cranmer, for most of the reformers' liturgies already included them.

Although the bread and wine were referred to only once at the offertory in the first book, even this was too much for the reformers. Therefore, in the 1552 Prayer Book no reference at all was made to the bread and wine, which in the early Church had been the only reason for having the offertory. The offertory was now strictly concerned with the giving of the people's alms. The new book further acceded to the radical reformers by deleting prayers for the departed in the Prayer for the Church and by drastically changing the sentences used at the distribution of Communion. In the 1549 book the archbishop had simply translated into English the traditional communion sentences, "The Body of our Lord Jesus Christ. . . . The Blood of our Lord Jesus Christ. . . ." The reformers were loud in their dismay over these sentences because for them these sentences emphasized the eucharistic presence of Christ. Therefore, in the 1552 book Cranmer used new sentences: "Take and eat this. . . . Drink this in remembrance. . . ."

To the services of Morning and Evening Prayer, Cranmer added a penitential beginning—Opening Sentence, General Confession, and Absolution—in order to bring these services into line with the reformers' emphasis upon sin and repentance in worship. The services of Baptism and Confirmation in the 1549 book were sorely lamented by the reformers; they especially disliked the number of traditional ceremonies that Cranmer had kept in these services. Thus, in the 1552 book he expunged all ceremonies from these services with the exception of the sign of the cross in Baptism and the laying on of the bishop's hands in Confirmation. The reformers had demanded the deletion of the cross in Baptism also, but here Cranmer stood his ground and retained this ancient part of the service. However, Cranmer moved the signing of the cross on the forehead from its traditional place in the beginning of the service to a point after the candidate had been baptized.

This moving around of traditional elements in the services (such as the cross in Baptism and the Gloria in the Eucharist) did cause confusion and fragmentation in the services of the second book. Yet Cranmer apparently knew what he was doing. He sought to retain in the liturgy those elements that he thought were traditional and necessary but which the radical reformers disliked. By deleting some things and moving others to new places, he sought to placate all concerned. For example, the radical reformers opposed the Prayer of Humble Access (We do not presume to come to this thy Table, etc.) because of its emphasis on Christ's eucharistic presence. Not only had Cranmer composed this prayer, but it also expressed his belief in the Lord's presence at the Communion. Thus, he would not delete the prayer, but for various reasons he placed it earlier in the service (in a place after the Sanctus) where liturgically it did not belong. That the Lord's Prayer should not be used in public worship was another view and demand of the reformers. Cranmer refused to accept this, but he changed the place of the prayer to a point after the Communion. (The American Prayer Book has in this century restored the Lord's Prayer and the Prayer of Humble Access to their original place just before Communion.) The reformers also criticized the Prayer of Thanksgiving, which the archbishop had composed, because it, too, expressed a belief in Christ's eucharistic presence. Cranmer also refused to delete this prayer, but he did provide an alternate prayer which could be used in its place.

Kneeling to receive the sacrament of Holy Communion was particularly repugnant to the radical English Protestants. They struggled fiercely to keep kneeling out of the 1552 book, but at the insistence of Archbishop Cranmer and his friend Bishop Ridley, kneeling for Communion was retained in the book. Parliament sanctioned the book in April of 1552, but it was not to be put into use until November 1, 1552. During the intervening months the extreme reformers John Knox and Bishop Hooper pleaded with King Edward, Protector Warwick, and the king's council to change the book and to forbid kneeling at Communion. When it appeared that the efforts of Hooper and Knox would succeed, Cranmer used all his ecclesiastical power and ingenuity to prevent such a result. When his first argument—that no change could be made in the book because Parliament had already passed it—did not move the king, Cranmer offered to write a rubric about the meaning of kneeling and place it at the end of the Communion Service in the Prayer Book. The government accepted this, and Cranmer wrote his famous Black Rubric, which has caused much controversy in Anglicanism ever since. Actually, the Black Rubric is not as "evil" as many have supposed. It did not forbid kneeling; in fact it supported kneeling. The rubric clearly denied that kneeling for Communion had anything to do with the medieval doctrine of Transubstantiation; it denied that Christ is physically or naturally present in the bread and wine. However, many Anglicans then and now held the same view, that Christ is not physically present in the species of bread and wine. Cranmer's positive contribution in the matter of the Black Rubric has often been overlooked. Mainly through his efforts and his rubric, kneeling for Communion was retained in Anglican worship.

It is rather clear that Cranmer's shifting around of various parts of the services was motivated by his principle of producing a liturgically conservative and doctrinally moderate Prayer Book. He sacrificed some, but not all, of his liturgical conservatism in the second book, but he did hold, particularly in his displacing of things, to a doctrinally moderate liturgy. Unfortunately the result of the archbishop's attempt to please all the religious and political parties in England at the time produced a Prayer Book which was too fragmented and confusing to be acceptable to very many people either at that time or in our age.

Chapter

The English Prayer Book

ALTHOUGH CREATED within a temporary political and ecclesiastical atmosphere, the 1552 Prayer Book became and remained the basis for all later Anglican Prayer Books well into the twentieth century. The present Church of England, for example, officially uses a seventeenth-century revision of the 1552 book; yet as shall be revealed, the seventeenth-century book was no more than a new edition of the 1552 book. Prayer Book revisions in the twentieth century by the autonomous branches of the Anglican Communion (as in the United States, Scotland, South Africa, Ceylon and India, Canada, and Ireland) have moved away, sometimes radically, from the 1552 book. Some of the recent Anglican revisions have added elements to the services (chiefly from the 1549 book or from the early church liturgies) or have deleted elements from Cranmer's second Prayer Book; but the working model for these revisions has been the 1552 book. How Cranmer's second book became the determining factor of Anglican worship for hundreds of years is an engrossing story involving historical circumstances and accidents.

The 1552 book remained the official liturgy of England for less than a year after it was put into use on November 1. The young King Edward VI died in July, 1553, and the new monarch, Queen Mary, was a Roman Catholic. In her brief five-year reign, Mary restored England to papal obedience, married a Spanish Catholic prince, and burned at the stake over three hundred Protestants, including Cranmer, Ridley, Latimer, and Hooper. The faithful Catholic queen also succeeded in restoring the doctrine, hierarchy, and Latin services of the Roman Church. Cranmer's second liturgy was proscribed by Mary's first Parliament in October of 1553, but even before the official act many parish churches and university chapels had returned to the Latin services. In point of time Cranmer's second book had a shorter official life in England than his first book of 1549.

Although the 1552 book soon became a dead liturgy in England (it may have been used in remote areas of the country during Mary's reign), it did remain a living liturgy on the European continent. At Mary's accession to the throne, and throughout her reign, a number of English Protestants, both clergy and laity, fled their homeland and sought refuge on the Continent because of religious persecution in England. Since Roman Catholic France was having troubles with the Protestant Huguenots, she had no desire to welcome the English exiles. The German Lutheran states also showed little interest in the fleeing English Protestants because the Lutherans had grown wary of the Swiss tendencies in English reformed Christianity. Most of the exiles were forced, therefore, to settle in the free cities of Frankfurt or Strasbourg, whereas a few, especially young clergy, went to the centers of continental Protestantism, Zwinglian Zurich or Calvinist Geneva. The largest group of religious exiles, something over two hundred, settled in Frankfurt. These refugees firmly intended to establish a Church of England in exile and to use the 1552 Prayer Book in public worship. At first they were impeded in their efforts to use the English liturgy because of the strong Calvinist outlook of the political and religious leaders of the city. After they had overcome this problem through persuasion and dogged determination, the exiles faced an even more formidable obstacle in the person of John Knox.

Knox's fiery preaching and natural ability for leadership had won for him the position of chief minister and leader of the English congregation in Frankfurt. But Knox, a strong Calvinist, had only contempt for the English Prayer Book. At the insistence of the congregation, Knox did consent to use the 1552 book, but he strongly modified it in a Calvinist direction. (It is rather instructive for later understanding of English and American worship to observe what Knox chiefly disliked about the Prayer Book and omitted from the services: the Church Year, the General Confession, Sursum Corda, Lord's Prayer, Gloria in Excelsis, and the Litany. In other words he objected chiefly to the congregation's parts in the services. As we have seen, Knox's objections became a characteristic of all Protestant worship from the sixteenth century onward.)

Early in 1554 Richard Cox, Dean of Christ Church, Oxford, during Edward's reign and later Bishop of Ely in Elizabeth's reign, fled England with some friends and eventually migrated to Frankfurt. He and his friends immediately took Knox to task for omitting the congregation's responses in the services; in fact they began to reinstate them. After a few months of bickering, the Cox group succeeded, with the political aid of the city council, in driving Knox and his few followers out of the English Church and the city of Frankfurt. Knox's English disciples went to Geneva or Zurich, where they became firmly converted, liturgically and doctrinally, to the continental Reformation. These two groups of English exiles, the Prayer Book party in Frankfurt and Strasbourg and the more extreme English reformers who went to Zurich and Geneva, became significant figures in the establishment of the Anglican Church in the reign of Elizabeth.

WORSHIP IN ELIZABETHAN ENGLAND

When Mary died in 1558 and Elizabeth became queen, she sought to restore the Catholic and reformed Church of England which had existed under her father, Henry, and her brother, Edward. At her accession, however, Elizabeth faced a personnel problem in the Church. All but one of the bishops from Mary's reign and many of the higher clergy—deans and canons of cathedrals, archdeacons, and university professors—refused to accept the restored Church of England and had to be deprived of their offices. Elizabeth, therefore, had to turn to the exiles in order to fill the higher offices and provide leadership for the Church. As they returned, some exiles brought with them the 1552 Prayer Book, which they desired to restore as the worship for the Church of England; yet other returning exiles, especially from Zurich and Geneva, sought to introduce the full reformed doctrine and liturgy of Swiss Protestantism. Thus, although the second Prayer Book had been considered a more extreme Protestant liturgy at its inception in 1552, by 1559 it had achieved a moderate position between the Latin Roman services of Mary's reign and the demands for a more reformed worship by the exiles returning from Switzerland. Since moderation has always been a major characteristic of Anglicanism, the 1552 Prayer Book was on its way to becoming the basis for Anglican worship.

If Elizabeth could have had her own way at the meeting of her first Parliament in the spring of 1559, there probably would not have been a new Act of Uniformity with a new

Prayer Book. Although a complex subject, Elizabeth's approach to religion appears to have been like her father Henry's: conservative, antipapal, and looking toward the establishment of a national Catholic Church. Yet Elizabeth did like her worship in English, and she preferred the first Prayer Book of 1549. At her accession Elizabeth allowed the substitution of English for Latin in some of the services and ordered the deletion of some ceremonies such as the elevation of the Host during the eucharistic Prayer of Consecration. By this action she hoped that for a while the English Church and nation would accept liturgical diversity in public worship. She remembered the liturgical experimentation which had taken place in Edward's reign from 1547-1549. Out of this diversity Elizabeth hoped that an English Prayer Book like that of 1549 would emerge.

The queen's hopes in the matter of worship were never realized. In 1559 the moderate Protestants, some of whom had been Frankfurt exiles, held the balance of political power. These moderates adamantly favored the 1552 book as the best means of establishing uniform public worship in England. Thus a new Act of Uniformity with a Prayer Book attached was passed by Parliament in the spring of 1559, and since she really had no choice, the queen gave her assent.

Except for a dozen or so differences, the Elizabethan 1559 Prayer Book was in order and content identical to the 1552 book. Three of the differences, all obviously dictated by Elizabeth and by those who thought as she did, have had an abiding influence on Anglican worship. Two of these were doctrinal and attempted to re-emphasize an Anglican approach to the eucharistic presence of Christ. First, the so-called Black Rubric of the 1552 book was deleted altogether. Second, the sentences used for the administration of the Holy Communion in the 1549 book—"The Body of our Lord Jesus Christ. . . . The Blood of our Lord Jesus

Christ. . . ."—were combined with the 1552 sentences: "Take and eat this in remembrance. . . . Drink this in remembrance. . . ." Thus, the present sentences of administration in Anglican liturgies represent a conflation of the 1549 and 1552 sentences. This conflation restated in more positive terms the traditional belief in the sacramental presence of Christ in the bread and wine, which had been weakened by the communion sentences in the 1552 book.

A small but significant change was made in the Litany. Cranmer wrote into his first English litany of 1544 a strongly antipapal suffrage, which he continued in the first two Prayer Books: "from the tyranny of the Bishop of Rome and all his detestable enormities. . . . Good Lord, deliver us." The queen had this suffrage expunged from the 1559 book. Perhaps more than any other Englishman at the time, Elizabeth realized that the greatest threat to a unified Church of England and a religious settlement in the realm would come from the extremes: the conservative Catholics and radical Protestants, now called Puritans. The official religion during the previous reign had been Roman Catholicism. The queen knew, therefore, that there was a significant Roman Catholic minority in England. These subjects she was not going to insult by allowing a strongly antipapal suffrage to remain in English worship. Yet at the other extreme were the returning English exiles from Geneva and Zurich who were ready to act for the establishment of a full continental Protestant Church along Swiss lines.

In many ways Elizabeth resembled Cranmer in her approach to the situation. She sought to establish a single and unified Anglican Church which would embrace as many Englishmen as possible. Like Cranmer, Elizabeth believed that a strong unified Church was essential for the peace and well-being of England at home and abroad. Cranmer, the statesman and archbishop, and Elizabeth, the monarch and the supreme governor of the Church, both believed that religion and politics were inseparable. Both shared a common understanding of the means to achieve political and ecclesiastical unity. They realized that the various theological opinions in England precluded a doctrinal settlement or English confession of faith. The means of unity for both was through worship in the Book of Common Prayer. However, what for Cranmer had been only an ideal became a reality during the long reign of Elizabeth. She claimed that she would make no window into a man's heart in order to learn about his beliefs as long as he and all Englishmen worshiped each Sunday and holy day in their parish church using the Book of Common Prayer.

The queen's principles were tested, but they endured and brought positive results. The English Roman Catholics sought excuses to remain away from Anglican worship; they attended, when possible, the services of wandering popish priests who had come from the Continent. The papists in England, however, were never strong enough numerically or politically to be more than a psychological threat to the Elizabethan establishment of Anglicanism. It was the militant Catholic power of Spain which really precipitated the Romish fears of Elizabethan Englishmen.

The extreme Protestants, or Puritans, openly attacked the Prayer Book. They opposed kneeling for Communion, the observance of holy days and saints' days, the service of the Communion of the Sick (they said it amounted to a private Mass), the signing of the cross upon the newly baptized in the baptismal service, the use of the ring in the marriage service, and the service for the Burial of the Dead. The Puritans labeled the Prayer Book "an imperfect book culled and picked out of that popish dunghill the Masse book full of all abominations." Actually the Puritans were working zealously for the abrogation of the Prayer Book, usually in order to replace it with free worship.

The Puritan program never succeeded in Elizabethan England. First the queen and eventually the bishops stoutly defended the English liturgy. As the reign progressed, the book was enforced and used more and more in the parish churches, so that by the queen's death in 1603, most Englishmen had been worshiping with the same Prayer Book for over forty years. Time as well as persuasion and force was making the Book of Common Prayer an accepted tradition in England.

ANGLICAN WORSHIP IN THE SEVENTEENTH CENTURY

When Elizabeth died in January, 1603, King James VI of Scotland was called southward and became King James I, the new monarch of England. Since James had been a Presbyterian in Scotland, the English Puritans believed that James' succession to the English throne signaled a new day for reformation of the English Church. As he journeyed southward to his coronation, the Puritans presented the king with a bold petition for further changes in the Church of England, especially in the matter of public worship. The English Puritans did not realize, however, that James had grown weary of the Presbyterians in Scotland. Like the English Puritans, the Scottish Presbyterian Church placed many strictures on the kind of life James sought to enjoy, especially his penchant for feasting and for participating in sports on Sunday.

Since the king did not want to alienate any of his new subjects, James did acknowledge the Puritans' petition. He called a conference at Hampton Court in January, 1604, at which representatives of the Puritan cause within the Church of England were invited to debate their petition with some bishops and other scholars of the Established Church. At the outset of the conference, King James joined vigorously with the Anglican bishops in refusing to accept the Puritan demands, and the debate at Hampton Court became exceedingly one-sided.

However, as a sop to some of the Puritans' minor complaints against the Prayer Book and in order to satisfy the wishes of some of the Anglican divines, the king and the bishops brought out a new edition of the Prayer Book. This 1604 Prayer Book was basically the 1552 book with the few changes of 1559 and with some further minor additions. These included some prayers in the Order for Morning Prayer, an instruction on the meaning of the sacraments in the Catechism, and the printing of titles to certain parts of various services. With the possible exception of the instruction on the sacraments, none of the 1604 additions was very significant. The 1604 Prayer Book, like the 1559 Elizabethan book, was not a revision but just a new edition of 1552.

Seventeenth-century Anglicanism has always been famous for her Laudian and Caroline divines. These divines were parish clergy, university professors, and bishops who greatly influenced the life of the Church of England during the episcopate of William Laud (he became a bishop in 1621 and was Archbishop of Canterbury from 1633 to 1645), and during the reigns of the two famous English kings of the century, Charles I (who reigned from 1625 to 1649) and his son Charles II (who reigned in exile from 1649 to 1660 and as the English monarch from 1660 to 1685). These Laudian and Caroline divines are usually called High Churchmen, which in seventeenth-century terms meant that they held a high doctrine of the Church, sacraments, and ministry. In the seventeenth century the High Churchmen generally believed that the visible Church on earth, the sacraments, and the ministry were of divine origin and ordinance, and were to be taken very seriously. The Low Churchmen generally believed that the visible Church, the ministry, and the observance of sacraments were of human creation. Although they did not take these things lightly, the Low

Churchmen emphasized a strict morality, personal piety, and charitable good works.

With few exceptions the Laudian High Churchmen were not interested in liturgical study or Prayer Book revision. They were quite content to accept the 1552 book as it had been slightly modified in 1559 and 1604. The Laudians, however, were sacramentalists, and they sought changes in the pattern of worship in the English churches. Since the 1550's the regular pattern of Sunday worship had been Morning Prayer, the Litany, and Ante-Communion, with the full Communion Service used only four times a year. The Laudians succeeded in having the full Communion Service more often, in many places at least once a month and in some churches and cathedrals even more frequently.

During the Laudian period most Anglican liturgical development took place in Scotland. In 1610 King James had forced the Presbyterian Church of Scotland to accept bishops. Then the king sought to make the Scottish Church accept the English Prayer Book, but by 1619 the Scots had accepted no more than a slight revision of their traditional Book of Common Order. Although the large majority of Scottish people were quite happy with their Church and liturgy, in the 1620's and 1630's a small group of Scots led by two bishops, John Maxwell and James Wedderborn, began to agitate for liturgical revision. Archbishop Laud cautioned them to be very careful and to seek nothing more radical than the English Book of Common Prayer. But the Anglican Prayer Book was too reformed and Protestant for these Scots, and led by Wedderborn, they produced a Prayer Book much like, but even more traditionally Catholic than, Cranmer's first book of 1549. Laud warned the king not to promulgate such a radical liturgy for the Church of Scotland, but Charles refused to heed the archbishop and authorized this Scottish Prayer Book in 1637.

The king's action immediately precipitated a religious

war between Scotland and England, which in turn led to the
political-religious civil war in England during the 1640's. As
a result of these wars, Archbishop Laud was beheaded in
1645, King Charles I was beheaded in January, 1649, and the
English monarchy was proscribed. From 1649 to 1660 England was a commonwealth under the somewhat dictatorial
leadership of Oliver Cromwell. Since the Anglican Church
and its Book of Common Prayer were also proscribed, official
English religion during the commonwealth period involved
an established but loosely organized Presbyterian-Independent Church which tended to tolerate all forms of Christianity
except Anglicanism and Roman Catholicism.

English worship during the Cromwellian period was
based on *A Directory for the Public Worship of God,* authorized by Parliament. Although chiefly a book of suggestions
with some rubrics or directions for public worship, in reality
the *Directory* became an English experiment in free worship.
The *Directory* represented the prime example and triumph
of the old Puritan approach to worship. For example, it
forbade the use of the Apocrypha; the sign of the cross in
Baptism; the wedding ring; the Church Year; vestments;
the service for the Burial of the Dead; Communion of the
Sick; the Gloria Patri, Te Deum, and Benedicite in Morning
Prayer; and the Creed, Preface, Sanctus, and Lord's Prayer
in the Holy Communion. In fact with the exception of singing Psalms in meter, the *Directory* forbade or discouraged
any congregational participation in the public worship of the
Church.

After Oliver Cromwell died in September, 1658, his experiment in commonwealth fell on bad days for lack of
leadership, and in May, 1660, the monarchy was restored to
England through a coalition of Presbyterians and Anglicans.
The restoration of the monarchy in the person of Charles
II led also to the enthusiastic restoration of the Anglican

Church and the Book of Common Prayer as the lawfully established Church and liturgy of England. The Presbyterians, who had aided the political restoration of the monarchy, had hoped to forestall the restoration of Anglicanism. However, since they had not endeared themselves politically or religiously to the English nation during the commonwealth period, and since the king, his advisers, and a majority of the members of the newly elected Parliament favored the establishment of Anglicanism, the Presbyterians' hopes were quickly defeated.

In order to restore the Prayer Book legally, the Parliament had to pass a new Act of Uniformity which, following the tradition of the sixteenth century, demanded that a new Prayer Book be appended to it. A liturgical commission was given the task of drawing up a new book. A small minority of these clergy, led by Bishops John Cosin and Matthew Wren, desired to make a thorough Catholic revision of the Anglican liturgy using the 1637 Scottish Prayer Book and the 1549 Prayer Book as sources. Another small minority sought real revision but along Presbyterian lines. The large majority of the commission, however, as well as the king and Parliament, pressed vigorously for the status quo. They wanted no revisions which would cause excitement, debate, or upheaval. Thus, the new Prayer Book drawn up by the commission, passed by the church convocation, and authorized by Parliament and king, was simply another edition of the 1552 Prayer Book.

The new edition, known today as the 1662 Prayer Book, actually contained over six hundred changes from the 1604 edition, but most were minor alterations in language and additional rubrical directions. (Many clergy and their congregations had forgotten how things had been done in the services before the commonwealth period.) Three additions in the 1662 book are worth mentioning because of their enduring influence. As something of an "olive branch" to the Presbyterians, a reworded Black Rubric on the meaning of kneeling for Communion was restored to the Prayer Book. The new rubric, even more broadly worded than Cranmer's, could support many interpretations of Christ's presence in the sacrament except the medieval doctrine of Transubstantiation.

Two significant additions were made to the Communion Service. At the offertory a new rubric ordered the priest to place the bread and wine upon the altar at that time. In other words, although almsgiving continued to be the main emphasis of the offertory, an idea of the traditional eucharistic offering of bread and wine was restored to its proper place. In the Prayer for the Church a commemorative intercession for the departed was also restored. Both of these additions were based on Cranmer's first English book of 1549, but the immediate influence for them came from the 1637 Scottish Prayer Book. That 1637 book, although it was never used as an official liturgy and in its own day caused rebellions and wars, has had a considerable influence on later Anglican liturgies. We have seen that a few of its ideas were incorporated in the 1662 English book, and we shall see that it influenced the later Prayer Books of the Episcopal Church of Scotland and the American Episcopal Church.

THE ENGLISH PRAYER BOOK TODAY

The 1662 Prayer Book has remained the official Book of Common Prayer in the Church of England to this day; yet its basic structure and content came from Cranmer's second Prayer Book. Despite new editions in 1559, 1604, and 1662, the Prayer Book of 1552 remained almost completely intact; it had become the basis for almost all later Anglican Prayer Books.

With the exception of a brief and unsuccessful attempt toward the end of the seventeenth century by a few Puritan bishops, no serious effort was made to revise the 1662 Prayer Book until the present century. The civil government represented the major deterrent to any change in liturgy. Since the Church of England is legally established, nothing in the Church could be revised without the consent of Crown and Parliament. This factor continued to be a stumbling block to the Church of England in this century, for by the early part of this century, strong agitation had grown in England for a revision of the official seventeenth-century liturgy.

Two rather different groups within the Church of England were calling for Prayer Book reform. One of these groups consisted of Anglicans who had become part of the Oxford Movement. From its inception in the 1830's, this movement was always basically doctrinal, emphasizing the historic Catholic nature of the Anglican Church, sacraments, and ministry. The Oxford Movement's strong concern for sacraments and sacramental worship led its proponents by the end of the last century to agitate for Prayer Book revision. For these Oxford Movement Anglicans, the Catholic nature of the sacraments was not adequately presented by Cranmer's sixteenth-century reformed services.

At the same time, however, there were Anglicans not at all sympathetic to the Oxford Movement who also demanded Prayer Book revision. These clergy and laity believed that the Church of England was living in the past and not meeting the needs of the emerging industrial society in late-nineteenth- and early-twentieth-century England. For them, Anglican worship as set forth in the 1662 Prayer Book well exemplified the Church's lack of contemporary relevance.

In 1904 a Royal Commission on Ritual Matters was convened, which strongly urged Prayer Book revision. However, the controversial nature of liturgical revision, con-

stitutional changes taking place in the English Church, and
the outbreak of war in 1914 forced the liturgical commission
to proceed very slowly. Thus, it was not until the 1920's
that a revised Prayer Book had been drawn up and offered
for discussion.

This proposed book valiantly attempted to blend the old
and the new. The major influences upon it were the 1549
book; early church, Eastern, and Scottish liturgies; and
modern liturgical ideas. In 1927 the Convocation of Clergy
and the Church Assembly, which included a House of Laity,
received, debated, and overwhelmingly approved the proposed revision. When the new Prayer Book went to Parliament in 1927, the House of Lords also passed it by a large
majority, but the book was rejected in the House of Commons by thirty-three votes—238 to 205. A slightly altered
version was submitted to Parliament in 1928, but it, too,
was defeated by the House of Commons.

Many of the members of Parliament who voted against
the book were not Anglicans, some not even Christians.
Many M.P.'s had been swayed by the minority extremes
within the Church of England—the Anglo-Catholics and
the Evangelicals. The extreme groups had campaigned vigorously against the revised book because it did not contain
enough—and in some cases contained very little—of what
they wanted in a Prayer Book. Parliament's rejection of the
revised Prayer Book immediately precipitated liturgical
chaos in the Church of England. Although the 1662 was the
official book, it was frequently not used as a whole; alterations and additions were made by local clergy. In the early
thirties the defeated revision of 1927-28 was somewhat extra-
legally sanctioned by a majority of bishops, and the proposed book was used sometimes as a whole, more often in
part or in conjunction with the 1662 book.

Since the Second World War, the impetus of the liturgical

movement and the dismay brought about by liturgical confusion in England have again caused clamor for Prayer Book
revision. However, a new approach to liturgical revision is
being attempted. Instead of having a liturgical commission
draw up a fully revised Prayer Book and then present it to
Parliament for approval, the Church of England has gained
legal sanction to experiment with various revised services
on the local parish level. In March, 1965, Parliament passed,
and the queen gave assent to, The Prayer Book (Alternative
and Other Services) Measure. This act makes provision for
the Church of England to experiment with alternative forms
for the present services in the Prayer Book and for the
creation and experimental use of services not now provided
in the Prayer Book. Already the Church of England's Liturgical Commission (which has been at work for several
years) has published, upon recommendation of the Arch-
bishops of Canterbury and York, two series of alternative
services. It is likely that in this year, 1966, at least some of
this material will be allowed for experimental use in the
local parishes.

The Church seeks to have liturgical experiment carried
out in all parishes for a definite period (the parliamentary
act allows a rather lengthy sixteen years) in order that the
whole Church can have opportunity to accept or reject the
revised services. If the Church as a whole generally accepts
these services, they will be presented to Parliament on
behalf of the whole Church. It is hoped that this so-called
grass-roots movement will mitigate the lobbying and rancor
which prevailed in the parliamentary debates and votes of
1927-28.

Chapter 9

The American Prayer Book

ALL THE AUTONOMOUS branches of the Anglican Communion have initiated Prayer Book revision in the twentieth century. Although in one way or another these churches began with the 1552 Prayer Book as their basic liturgy, the revisions have been greatly influenced by four sources: the proposed English book of 1927-28, the Scottish liturgies of the seventeenth to nineteenth centuries, Cranmer's first English book of 1549, and the early Eastern and Western church liturgies. The Scottish liturgies demand some comment, particularly because of their vast influence on the American Episcopal Prayer Book.

THE SCOTTISH BACKGROUND

The Episcopal Church in Scotland has always been numerically one of the smallest independent branches of the Anglican Communion; yet from the seventeenth to the

136

twentieth century, this Church stood out as the leader of liturgical study and influence within Anglicanism. We have already noted something of the nature and influence of the 1637 Scottish Prayer Book. In the eighteenth century, since the tiny and struggling Episcopal Church in Scotland was free from state control (the officially established Church of Scotland was and is Presbyterian), many of her bishops and other scholars immersed themselves in liturgical study and experiments in worship.

The chief influence and model in all their studies was the 1637 book. The Scottish Episcopalians never used the book officially, apparently because of the clamor and war it had caused in Scotland and England in the previous century, and because copies of it were scarce in the eighteenth century. It would have cost the small Church too much to reprint; thus, the Scottish Church officially used the English Prayer Book, ample copies of which were sent to Scotland by friends south of the border.

In addition to the 1637 Prayer Book, the Scots studied Cranmer's first book of 1549 and especially the Eastern liturgies. Greek influence became especially evident in the Scots' approach to the Prayer of Consecration in the Communion Service. Following the Greek East rather than Cranmer's 1549 book, the Scots restored an invocation of the Holy Spirit to the Prayer of Consecration, placing the invocation in the Eastern position after the words of institution. The Scots also accepted the Greek idea that the invocation of the Holy Spirit should be upon the bread and wine that "they may become" the Body and Blood of Christ. Study of the early church liturgies also influenced the Scottish Episcopalians to restore an offering of the bread and the cup, which Cranmer had eliminated from the Prayer of Consecration even in 1549.

The chief concern of Scottish liturgical scholars was the

Holy Communion Service. From time to time throughout the eighteenth century, these scholars would publish in pamphlet form their ideas for improving this service in relation to the English Prayer Book. These pamphlets, which the Scots called "Wee Bookies" because they could easily be inserted into the Prayer Book, were distributed to a small group of parishes for experimental use. The most significant of the Wee Bookies was published in 1764 by two Scottish bishops. This eucharistic liturgy (which is the basis of the eucharistic service in the present Prayer Book of the Scottish Church) was known to the first bishop of the American Episcopal Church, Samuel Seabury, and was brought by him to America after his consecration in Scotland in 1784.

THE FIRST AMERICAN PRAYER BOOK

Before the American Revolution, the Church of England in colonial America was not a strong Church. It had a small membership in comparison with other Christian churches. An Anglican minority in most colonies was hardly surprising since, with the exception of Virginia, many of the American colonies had been founded by those who dissented from, and who had been persecuted by, the established Church of England.

During the colonial period this tiny Anglican Church remained a disorganized and disunited Church, chiefly because the highly structured Church of England never organized the Anglicans in America. No dioceses were created, no bishop was ever sent to the American colonies. All Anglicans in the colonies were nominally under the jurisdiction of the Bishop of London, who usually did little to aid a flock so far away. Some semblance of organization for the American Anglicans was provided by the private missionary Society for the Propagation of the Gospel in Foreign Parts (S.P.G.), which attempted to send clergy, money, and ecclesiastical supplies for the Church in America.

Without dioceses and bishops, the Anglicans in colonial America tended to organize along congregational lines. The local unit or parish became their chief concern. In a given colony some Anglican clergy and laymen might evidence interest and concern for other Anglicans in the same colony, but there was little communication with, or interest in, Anglicans outside one's colony. Nevertheless, there was one element of unity throughout the Anglican Church in America, and typically it was worship. Almost all the Anglican parishes used the English Prayer Book in public worship. In the earliest days of colonial America, the 1604 book provided the means for Anglican worship, but from the 1660's until the Revolution the 1662 Prayer Book was used. As has happened so often in the history of Anglicanism, the public worship of the Book of Common Prayer provided the only visible means of church order and unity.

During the Revolution some Anglicans vigorously supported the British army; others joined the revolutionary cause. When the war ended and the American colonies became an independent nation, many of the Anglican clergy and laity who had supported the British cause left the United States and returned to England or migrated to Canada. A Church, then, which had been somewhat small in numbers before the Revolution was even smaller after the war. Furthermore, since the colonies had separated from England and had become a sovereign nation, it was both natural and necessary that the Anglican Church in America separate from the mother Church of England. Thus, the Protestant Episcopal Church in the United States became the first independent branch of the Anglican Communion.

Like the new young nation, the Episcopal Church in America encountered great difficulties at first in organizing and establishing herself. The first significant efforts toward organization began in 1784. A majority of the clergy in Connecticut met and elected Samuel Seabury to be bishop of the Episcopal Church in that state. Seabury journeyed to England for consecration, but the English bishops had little interest in consecrating him. Consequently they found a number of reasons in canon law and civil law to support their refusal to consecrate. Seabury then went to Scotland; was well received by the Scottish episcopate; was consecrated on November 14, 1784; and thus became the first American Episcopal bishop. At his consecration Seabury made a concordat with the Scottish bishops in which he agreed to make the worship of the Church in Connecticut similar to the worship of the Episcopal Church in Scotland. To this end he took home with him the Scottish Wee Bookie of 1764.

Just a month before Seabury's consecration in Scotland, a convention composed of clergy and lay delegates from Episcopal churches in New York, New Jersey, Pennsylvania, Delaware, and Maryland met in New York. This convention accomplished little except to call, and provide some means of organization, for a general convention of the Episcopal Church to meet in 1785. The convention of 1785 turned out not to be very "general." Only seven states were represented —the five from the previous year together with Virginia and South Carolina. No Episcopal delegations came from the New England states or from Georgia and North Carolina, for Episcopalians in these states were not yet ready to unite with the others in a national Episcopal Church.

The 1785 convention drew up, however, a proposed new Prayer Book for the Protestant Episcopal Church in America. This proposed book, like so many proposed liturgies in the history of Anglican worship, was rarely used in public worship; yet it had great influence on later Prayer Books. The 1785 book strongly influenced the first official American Prayer Book of 1789, and has continued to affect American worship to the present day.

A committee of the convention, which included four of

the leading Episcopal clergymen of the day—Samuel Provost of New York, William White of Pennsylvania, Charles Wharton of Delaware, and William Smith of Maryland—drew up the proposed book in five days, and won the convention's approval of the book within two more days. Although the 1662 English Prayer Book provided the basis for the committee's work, the proposed book turned out in a few significant points to be a radical departure from traditional Anglican liturgy and doctrine. The reason for this was not the committee's haste, but its written sources and the opinions of some of its members.

The committee possessed a group of works written in the seventeenth and eighteenth centuries by various English Presbyterians and Puritans, some of whom were Anglicans. These documents severely criticized the English Prayer Book along the usual Puritan lines. Since the opinions of the committee members generally agreed with these writings, some of the old Puritan ideas which had never been accepted in the English Prayer Books finally were adopted into the American proposed book of 1785. Thus, some of the congregation's responses in Morning and Evening Prayer were deleted, the sign of the cross in Baptism was made optional, and the services of Holy Matrimony and the Burial of the Dead were greatly shortened. Many of these Puritan ideas have remained in the various American Prayer Books; for example, the sign of the cross in Baptism was not made mandatory until the last Prayer Book revision in 1928, and the Order for Morning Prayer still lacks some of the congregation's responses found in the English Prayer Book.

Another set of documents before the committee consisted of some official resolutions on liturgical reform from the state conventions of Massachusetts and Virginia, which had met prior to the 1785 convention. The Virginia resolutions were presented to the committee by its delegation, but since Mas-

sachusetts sent no delegates to the 1785 convention, its resolutions were sent with accompanying interpretative letters
to William Smith, the committee's chairman. The tenor of
these documents revealed a bias against creeds, the basis of
which involved a growing anti-Trinitarianism on the part of
some Anglicans. In England and America before and after
the Revolution, the religious movements of Deism and Uni-
tarianism strongly affected contemporary Anglican theology
and worship. For example, the Anglican King's Chapel in
Boston became one of the first strong Unitarian churches in
America in 1786.

The results of this anti-Trinitarian outlook in the 1785
book included the deletion of the Nicene Creed from the
Prayer Book, the elimination of the "descent into hell" clause
from the Apostles' Creed in Morning and Evening Prayer,
and the prohibition of the Gloria Patri (Glory be to the
Father, and to the Son, and to the Holy Ghost, etc.) after the
canticles. The Gloria Patri was permitted only at the end
of the whole selection of Psalms, and not as in the English
Prayer Book after each Psalm. Moreover, the Athanasian
Creed, which in the English Prayer Book had always been
used on certain festivals in place of the Apostles' Creed, was
also deleted. Thus, the Apostles' Creed remained the only
creed in the 1785 proposed book. Although the Nicene Creed
was restored in the first American Prayer Book of 1789, the
Athanasian Creed has never been accepted into the American
Episcopal liturgy. Also, although the "descent into hell"
clause was returned to the Apostles' Creed, the American
Prayer Book still has a rubric providing for a substitute
clause, and the Gloria Patri remains optional after the canticles and at the end of each Psalm.

Despite the enduring influence of the 1785 proposed
book, it was rarely used in the early Episcopal Church. At
the state conventions held after the 1785 meeting, only Vir-

ginia ratified the proposed book; most of the other conventions rejected it as too radical, except South Carolina, which believed it had not gone far enough. The New York convention refused to deal with the book on the grounds that the English bishops were reviewing it at that time. The 1785 convention had sent its proposed liturgy to the English bishops in the hope that they would approve of it and then agree to consecrate some bishops for the American Church. The book greatly dismayed the English bishops, however, especially in the matter of the creeds. It was not until a further and again small convention of Episcopalians met in 1786 and promised to accept some of their criticisms of the proposed book that the English bishops consented to consecrate Americans to the episcopate. Thus, in 1787 William White of Pennsylvania and Samuel Provost of New York became the second and third bishops of the American Church.

By 1789 the forces of unity in the Episcopal Church had overcome some of the divisive elements, and the first General Convention of the Church, with delegations from each of the states, was held in Philadelphia. Naturally one of the convention's major tasks was to provide a Prayer Book for the Episcopal Church. Bishops Seabury and White as well as the Maryland priest William Smith, who had been committee chairman for the 1785 book, were chiefly responsible for the first official American Prayer Book. Although the 1662 English Prayer Book was again their working model, in many ways they accomplished one of the most incredible compromises in the history of Anglican worship. By acceding to Seabury's wishes and his Scottish source, the committee in some ways strongly returned the Communion Service to the Catholic tradition of Cranmer's 1549 book and to the early liturgies. The American book adopted the Scottish Prayer of Consecration in the Eucharist, with the exception that the wording of the invocation of the Holy Spirit was altered so as not to

petition explicitly for the change of the sacramental elements
into the Body and Blood of Christ. The 1789 Eucharistic
Prayer still remains in the American book.

Other Scottish influences, all in the Communion Service,
included optional allowance of the Summary of the Law
(Hear what our Lord Jesus Christ saith, etc.) after the Decalogue, the Gloria Tibi (Glory be to Thee, O Lord) before the
reading of the Gospel, and the elimination of the 1662 version of the Black Rubric about kneeling for Communion.

If Seabury's demands restored some elements of ancient
Catholic worship, the demands of White and Smith injected
many of the old Puritan liturgical ideas into the Prayer Book.
Most of the Puritan and some of the anti-Trinitarian elements
of the 1785 proposed book became part of the official 1789
Prayer Book. In fact, some of the Puritan ideas which had
failed to win acceptance in 1785 did make it into the 1789
book. For example, the Puritans always considered the Gospel canticles of Magnificat and Nunc Dimittis in Evening
Prayer to be popish, even though these canticles came from
the Gospel of Luke. The 1785 proposed book retained the
Magnificat and Nunc Dimittis, but they were eliminated
from the first official Prayer Book.

THE NINETEENTH CENTURY

The Prayer Book of 1789, a strange Catholic-Puri-
tan compromise, remained the liturgy of the Episcopal
Church for over one hundred years despite continued unhap-
piness about the book within the Church. During the nineteenth century the Episcopal Church was a bastion of arch-
conservatism in which change, revision, or innovation rarely
took place. Two major factors contributed to the Church's
outlook: the inherited traditionalism of Anglicanism and the
elements of discord and division which beset the American
Church through most of the century. There were High

Churchmen and Low Churchmen; after the 1840's there were Oxford Movement disciples, with their emphasis on Catholic doctrines and ritualism; there were social-ecclesiastical problems involving first the matter of the Episcopal Church moving out of the cities to rural and frontier America and then the matter of the Civil War. Moreover, there were divisions which had no doctrinal, liturgical, or social cause, but involved long-standing personal animosities between bishops and between the churches in the various states.

Naturally in the midst of such a situation, revision of the Prayer Book was not possible. In fact, as in sixteenth- and seventeenth-century England the Prayer Book became a symbol, even a means, of unity in the midst of discordant elements. This point is exemplified by the leading High Churchman of the early part of the century, John Henry Hobart, Bishop of New York. Hobart recognized the great doctrinal disunity in the young Episcopal Church; thus, he followed in the tradition of Cranmer, Elizabeth, and Laud by seeking unity within the Church through a common worship. Hobart strongly opposed Prayer Book revision; he believed that the Episcopal Church should unite through the worship of the Prayer Book established by the first General Convention.

Actually it took a clergyman, who though claimed by all elements of the Church was so unique that he belonged to none, to instigate the first change in the pattern of Episcopal worship in the nineteenth century. William Augustus Muhlenberg, Rector of the Church of the Holy Communion in New York City, sponsored a famous Memorial presented to the House of Bishops at the General Convention of 1853. The basic purpose of the Memorial was missionary and social, for Muhlenberg believed that the Episcopal Church neither reached out to, nor was understood by, many classes of American society. In the course of the Memorial, Muhlenberg protested that the centuries-old pattern of Anglican Sunday worship—which included Morning Prayer, the Litany, and Ante-Communion with the full Communion quarterly or monthly and with a sermon—did not reach out to or meet the needs of a growing industrial society.

Although the House of Bishops did little to implement the Memorial, the bishops did state officially what the Prayer Book had already provided in its rubrics—that Morning Prayer, the Litany, and Ante-Communion were separate services and did not have to be used all together on a Sunday morning. The Memorial and the bishops' statement immediately affected the pattern of worship. Most Episcopal churches established Morning Prayer and sermon as the regular Sunday worship, with the Holy Communion celebrated usually on the first Sunday of the month. In those few parishes where the Oxford Movement found acceptance, the Holy Communion became the regular service every Sunday.

Toward the end of the nineteenth century, another Episcopal clergyman who transcended the parties and interest groups then prevalent in the Church led the way to the first revision of the American Prayer Book at the General Convention of 1880. William Reed Huntington, Rector of Grace Church in New York, succeeded in winning acceptance for the establishment of a committee of bishops, presbyters, and laymen to determine what alterations were needed in the Prayer Book. Huntington's resolution stated his chief reason for revision: that the Prayer Book was becoming less and less relevant to the changes and growth in American life at the end of the nineteenth century. Christian unity also occupied Huntington's thoughts. He believed that Anglicans and Episcopalians had made a fetish of liturgical uniformity, and that their insistence upon Sunday worship being the same service, done in the same way at the same hour in all churches, would hinder the Episcopal Church's contribution to Christian unity.

The committee established by Huntington's resolution experienced troublous times throughout the eighties. The prevailing attitude in the Church at the time forced the committee at its outset to promise not to make any major changes in the Communion Service and not to propose any revisions which would alter the traditional doctrinal standards of Anglicanism. If these prerequisites were not sufficiently crippling, the committee found that any alterations it proposed, no matter how minor, brought forth a wave of criticism from various segments of the Church. Through sheer perseverance, the committee eventually did produce a slightly revised Prayer Book which was authorized by the General Convention of 1892.

The 1892 Prayer Book hardly differed from the first book of 1789, but it did make a few significant alterations. It introduced a principle of flexibility into Episcopal worship by allowing under certain circumstances the omission of the penitential introduction to Morning and Evening Prayer. It permitted the Decalogue to be omitted from the Communion Service as long as it was read once on a Sunday. Other important changes were the restoration of the Gospel canticles of Magnificat and Nunc Dimittis to Evening Prayer and the provision for a second Eucharist on Christmas and Easter by adding a second Collect, Epistle, and Gospel for these festivals.

The 1892 revision achieved very little specifically in the matter of Prayer Book reform; yet from a long view it accomplished much for the development of worship in the Episcopal Church. No matter how little it was applied, the 1892 revision established the principle of flexibility in worship. Before the worship of the Church could ever move into the world of its day, this principle had to be stated and eventually accepted. Moreover, no matter how few and minor were the changes, the 1892 book proved that the Episcopal Church was capable of Prayer Book revision. Finally, so many Episcopalians were dissatisfied with the 1892 book because specific revisions were few, that in less than forty years a new, and eventually more thorough, revision was accomplished.

THE TWENTIETH CENTURY

Divisive elements within the Church continued into the present century, but they became far less influential and popular. The emergence of a liberal, or at least moderating, spirit precipitated by the world wars and the social problems of a complex industrial-scientific society moved the Church away from total immersion in strictly ecclesiastical matters. Church doctrine, discipline, and liturgy remained tremendously important, but more and more these ecclesiastical elements were being discussed within the context of American society and world affairs.

The effect of a moderating spirit on the worship of the Episcopal Church is illustrated by the acceptance throughout the Episcopal Church of one element proclaimed and fought for by the nineteenth-century Oxford Movement. The movement's strong emphasis upon sacramental doctrine, especially the Holy Communion, was primarily responsible for the institution of the early service of the Holy Communion on Sunday in most Episcopal parishes at the end of the last century or the beginning of this century.

A major liturgical accomplishment of the Episcopal Church occurred in 1928 when the General Convention authorized the present American Prayer Book. The Church's general dissatisfaction with the 1892 Prayer Book had moved the General Convention of 1913 to accept a Memorial from the Diocese of California and to establish a joint commission of bishops, presbyters, and laymen for the purpose of revising the Prayer Book. The commission worked carefully for over ten years, always seeking to keep the Church, especially the

General Convention, informed of what it was doing. Despite some agitation against the purpose of the commission and especially some of its proposals, the commission gained solid support by the 1920's. In 1925 the General Convention tentatively approved the new Prayer Book offered by the commission. Then the 1928 convention accepted, with a few minor changes, the commission's draft and made it the official worship of the Episcopal Church.

Many written sources and private opinions influenced the making of the present American Prayer Book. As in all recent Anglican revisions, the Scottish liturgies (especially the 1637 Prayer Book), the first English book of 1549, and the early church liturgies were carefully studied. Another prominent influence was the liturgical committee of the Church of England, which was working at the same time as the American commission. The American body kept in close touch with the ideas and proposals of its English counterpart, so that the English proposed book of 1927-28, which never won legal adoption at home, made its influence felt in America.

In addition to consulting ancient and English sources, the American commission strove valiantly to adapt the Church's traditional worship to the needs and purposes of a twentieth-century Church. The principle of flexibility begun by the 1892 revision was extended and deepened. More freedom to shorten or enrich the services was permitted throughout the book. For example, in the Holy Communion the Decalogue had only to be used once a month and the long exhortation but three times a year. Optional additions of a gradual hymn or anthem between the Epistle and Gospel, and the proclamation of the Laus Tibi (Praise be to thee, etc.) after the Gospel lesson were added. In Morning Prayer, seasonal invitatory antiphons before the Venite, and the use of the Lord's Prayer in the more traditional place after the creed, became new optional additions.

Although the 1928 book involved some alterations in all the services of the Prayer Book, much of the book's basic structure and content remained in the tradition of Cranmer's second book of 1552. The services of Morning Prayer and Holy Baptism in the present American book are practically identical to the English 1552 book. Only the Communion Service in the 1928 revision won some definite structural changes from the 1552 book. An actual offering of the bread and wine at the offertory before the elements were placed upon the altar was directed. The Prayer of Humble Access, which since 1552 in all English and American liturgies had remained after the Sanctus and before the Prayer of Consecration, was restored to its original place before the administration of Holy Communion. Moreover, the Lord's Prayer, which since Cranmer's second book had been said after the Communion, was also restored to its present place after the Prayer of Consecration. These changes, together with the American Prayer of Consecration, adopted from the Scots in 1789, have made the American Communion Service somewhat different from the traditional pattern established in 1552.

The 1928 American book was never considered the final achievement for worship in the Episcopal Church. The very convention of 1928 which authorized the present Prayer Book recognized this, and in a further action established a permanent commission—the Standing Liturgical Commission—of the convention. The Standing Commission's chief responsibility has been to make a continuing study of liturgy and worship, especially in dealing with the memorials and suggestions made to General Convention by dioceses, interest groups, and individuals. Yet the commission has not only studied; it has created. In the thirties the commission produced *The Book of Offices*, which contained "Services for certain occasions not provided in the Book of Common

Prayer." The General Convention of 1937 authorized this book for use in the Church; since then the conventions of 1946 and 1958 have authorized revised editions of *The Book of Offices.* This valuable work includes services for the adoption of children, the installation of a bishop, and the admission of wardens and vestrymen.

During the 1950's the commission began to publish the fruits of its two decades of liturgical study. Thus far, seventeen studies covering all services in the Prayer Book have been published by the Church Pension Fund in a series called *Prayer Book Studies.* The publication of these studies has coincided with a growing demand in the Church for a new major revision of the Prayer Book. The changing conditions wrought by a nuclear society seemed to call for a new Prayer Book for the second half of the twentieth century.

Although not opposed to Prayer Book revision, both the General Convention and the Standing Commission believed that the Church should allow time and thought before creating a new Prayer Book. As in the Church of England today, the Episcopal Church has come to realize that widespread study of, and experimentation with, proposed liturgical changes must precede any formulation and authorization of a new Prayer Book. Since the Episcopal Church lacked legal sanction for public liturgical experiment, the Liturgical Commission proposed to the General Convention of 1961 an amendment to the Constitution of the Protestant Episcopal Church which was accepted at that convention and then ratified and authorized at the convention of 1964. The amendment provides that any meeting of General Convention, through a majority vote of both the House of Bishops and House of Deputies, can "authorize for trial use throughout this Church, as an alternative at any time or times to the established Book of Common Prayer or to any section or Office thereof, a proposed revision of the whole Book or of any portion thereof, duly undertaken by the General Convention." Immediately upon ratification of this amendment in 1964, both houses of General Convention authorized a three-year trial use of *The Calendar and the Collects, Epistles, and Gospels for the Lesser Feasts and Fasts and for Special Occasions,* which is included in volume sixteen of the Liturgical Commission's *Prayer Book Studies.* Although the first authorized experiment in Episcopal Church worship involves a relatively minor matter, most churchmen concerned about liturgical reform have hailed the enabling amendment for trial use as the best means for meaningful and generally acceptable Prayer Book revision.

Chapter 10

Christian Worship Today

WORSHIP AND THE ECUMENICAL MOVEMENT

THE MAJOR ISSUES confronting Christian worship today are vividly clarified by viewing worship in its historical perspective, for the problems of worship today are not entirely new—in fact, contemporary liturgical issues have evolved from the total history of Christian worship. The two basic issues of worship today involve the ecumenical movement and Christian worship in a contemporary society.

In seeking ways to overcome the disunity of Christendom, the leaders of the ecumenical movement have recognized that worship has been a major cause of Christian division as well as a stumbling block to Christian unity. Nevertheless, some ecumenists believe that worship may become both the means and the expression of true Christian unity. Worship as a divisive force exists because within Christendom there

153

are churches with a strong tradition of liturgical uniformity and churches with an equally strong tradition of free worship. As we have seen, both traditions were born of the sixteenth-century Reformation.

In the early and medieval periods, Western Christianity blended a strong liturgical outlook with a real sense of freedom in worship. The outline or order of services became fixed rather early in the Church's history, but elements continued to be added throughout the patristic and medieval periods. By the early Middle Ages the content of the services was becoming fixed, yet additions and variations continued until the sixteenth century. In the High Middle Ages all areas of Western Christendom adopted the Roman services as the norm for worship; however, each area, whether England, France, Spain, northern Italy, or Germany, held to and even introduced its own regional variations. Furthermore, no pope, council, or parliament decreed or demanded a uniform liturgy. Thus, until the sixteenth century—when Anglicans, Roman Catholics, and to some extent Lutherans introduced a strict liturgical uniformity—there existed a true sense of liturgical form as well as freedom in Christian worship.

This liturgical freedom in pre-Reformation Christianity was, however, neither related to, nor similar to, that which developed in the free-worship churches of the Reformation and modern eras. Modern free-worship churches give final authority for worship in the local church to the minister and congregation. Forms of worship (such as the recent Book of Worship set forth by the 1964 General Conference of the Methodist Church in the United States) may be provided by other than local authorities, but the use of such forms is left to the discretion of the local minister and congregation. The pre-Reformation Church did not permit this kind of local or congregational freedom. The bishops, usually through the cathedral rites, determined the order and content of local usage. Yet the bishops often adopted the forms of worship from an area liturgical center such as the dioceses of Sarum in England, Milan in northern Italy, and Toledo in Spain. The pre-Reformation Church avoided, therefore, the two crucial problems of the free-worship churches: that often the local minister and congregation do not have the liturgical knowledge and competence to be the final authority in worship; and that such a system produces a vast diversity of worship within individual denominations and among the churches of Christendom.

The history of Christian worship offers to present-day discussion of Church unity three possibilities for the ordering of worship in a united Church: the regional liturgical freedom of early and medieval Christianity, the liturgical uniformity of Reformation Anglicanism and Romanism, or the free-worship approach of some Reformation and most modern Protestant churches. Of the three, liturgical uniformity has been discarded in all ecumenical discussions where organic union has at least reached the proposal stage. For example, the American Consultation on Church Union— which presently includes the African Methodist Episcopal Church, the Disciples of Christ, the Evangelical United Brethren Church, the Methodist Church, the Presbyterian Church in the U.S., the Protestant Episcopal Church, the United Church of Christ, and the United Presbyterian Church in the U.S.A.—has already in its short existence disavowed a strictly uniform worship. At its second meeting in Oberlin, Ohio, in March, 1963, the consultation adopted this principle: "The living Tradition of the church implies certain basic elements of Christian worship but does not confine worship to a single plan or form." (*Digest, Consultation on Church Union*, Vol. I-II, p. 48) [At its most recent meeting in May, 1966, at Dallas, Texas, the consultation reiterated its stand against a strictly uniform worship. In the Principles of

Church Union adopted at the meeting, it was decided that in the early life of a united Church each of the constituting churches would maintain its own tradition and forms of worship. In many ways the consultation seems to be following the South Indian approach, which is commented on below.] Furthermore, the official report of conversations between the Church of England and the Methodist Church in England states: ". . . there is no intention whatever of forcing those Methodists unaccustomed to liturgical forms to adopt the Book of Common Prayer." (*Conversations . . . A Report*, 1963, p. 49)

It is significant that Anglicans were assenting parties to both these statements. Anglicanism really created strict liturgical uniformity with the first English Prayer Book of 1549, and for several centuries uniformity of worship was a mainstay of Anglican unity. However, rapid changes in modern life, of which flexibility and diversification are major characteristics, have shown that the idea of Cranmer, Elizabeth, Laud, and Hobart is no longer viable. Unity does not depend on a tight uniformity, and in recent practice Anglicans themselves have not often adhered to their founding principle.

In matters of worship, as well as ministry, government, and doctrine, church-unity discussions today are greatly influenced by the Church of South India, a merger of Anglicans, Congregationalists, Methodists, and Presbyterians, which began in September, 1947. The South Indian Church's approach to worship is basically post-Reformation freedom. Its constitution states: "No forms of worship which before the Union have been in use in any of the uniting churches shall be forbidden in the Church of South India, nor shall any wonted forms be changed or new forms introduced into the worship of any congregation without the agreement of the pastor and the congregation." (*Constitution*, II, 12) Since the local minister and congregation are the final au-

thority for worship, the Church of South India did nothing
about liturgy and worship before its inception in 1947 except
to have a liturgical committee prepare a service of inaugura-
tion and some experimental services of ordination. By 1950,
however, some members of the new Church desired guidance
in liturgical norms, especially in the service of the Lord's
Supper. Thus, the liturgical committee reconvened, and after
experiment and revision produced a eucharistic service which
the C.S.I. Synod authorized for use in 1954. This service has
gained wide acclaim from liturgical scholars throughout the
world, chiefly because of its creative modernity in its attempt
to provide a liturgy for present-day India, and its success in
involving the congregation throughout the service.

After the eucharistic service the liturgical committee published for experimental use other services such as Baptism,
Marriage, etc. And in 1962 the synod gathered these services
together in the Book of Common Worship, which it authorized for use in the churches if the local minister and congregation so desire. However, since the South India prayer
book is regularly used in all the Church's theological schools,
and since the book is strongly supported by many of the
bishops, liturgical enthusiasts in the C.S.I. hope that the Book
of Common Worship will become widely accepted. At this
time it is too early to know whether their hopes will be realized, for the C.S.I. principle of free worship will always
encourage problems about whether the local minister and
congregation are sufficiently knowledgeable to be the final
judge of worship. Yet even more important, especially for
a united Church, is that free worship allows the possibility,
and usually the actuality, of a vast diversity in worship, especially in the local areas. It is difficult to see how true
Christian unity can be achieved unless Christians in local
areas can really (and one might say comfortably) worship
together.

This point is far more germane to Christian unity in

America and England than in South India, for Christianity in North America and Britain is the majority religion. Thus, Christian unity does not have the imperative it has in India; nor was the fragmentation of Christianity as great or as old in South India as it is in the Western world.

Since liturgical uniformity is unrealistic in contemporary Christianity and the free-worship principle presents obstacles to realistic Christian unity, the remaining alternative offered by the history of Christian worship—the regional liturgical freedom of early and medieval Christianity—may prove helpful to the ecumenical movement. For example, at the inception of a united Church a wide variety of liturgical forms and services would be provided by a liturgical commission. After a substantial but definite period of time for discussion of, and experiment with, the variety of forms, the highest governing body of the united Church would authorize a service book which would be the book of worship used in all congregations of the united Church. This service book, however, would be characterized by freedom, variety, and flexibility. At least two, and perhaps three or four, forms would be provided for the regularly used services. Provision should also be made for the use of extemporary prayer in all the services. The chief value of such a service book would be to establish what is basic and essential to the order and content of Christian worship in a united Church.

Such a solution would not be without problems, but it would seem to create less confusion and diversity than the free-worship principle, and would avoid strict liturgical uniformity. It would, however, include the positive elements from both the traditions of free worship and liturgical uniformity. Such a solution would not be identical to the regional liturgical freedom of early Christianity, but similar in that the services would be authorized by a higher authority than the local congregation, and a variety of rites or forms would be permitted.

Moreover, this kind of approach to ecumenical worship would be much more helpful in church-unity discussions with the Roman Catholic and Eastern Orthodox churches than would the free-worship approach. Anglicans and Protestants should be ever aware that any real Christian unity must inevitably include the Roman and Orthodox churches. Thus, whether the matter be doctrine, discipline, or worship, nothing should be done now in Anglican and Protestant unity plans which would lead these churches to greater separation from other branches of historic Christendom.

CHRISTIAN WORSHIP IN CONTEMPORARY SOCIETY: A THEOLOGICAL PROBLEM

The really crucial issue of worship today is related to that which dominates every aspect of Christianity—the desire for relevance. Is worship relevant to the culture and civilization of this time in the twentieth century? Since the relevance of all institutional aspects of the Church—doctrine, discipline, structure, and government—is being questioned, there is no reason why worship should not be similarly tested. The problem for Christian worship has been that in the last decade a few theologians, ecclesiastical leaders, and non-churchmen have taken a cursory glance at Christian worship and have decided it is irrelevant.

The history of Christian worship provides ample evidence that a cursory glance at worship could result in such a conclusion. For well over a thousand years in Christian history, the actual worship of the Church was often unimportant, at times even irrelevant. From the early Middle Ages to the Reformation, public worship became more and more clergy centered and controlled. The large majority of Christians— the laity—did not offer corporate worship together; they were spectators at the priest's worship. If lay people did worship, it was through personal devotions, not corporate liturgy. Instead of reforming the situation, the Protestant Reformation and Roman Catholic Counter Reformation only intensified it. In the Protestant churches the minister kept full control over the service from pulpit, reading desk, or table. The laity's function was to listen; corporate worship was not their prerogative. In the Roman Church, worship became even more priest centered than it had been in the Middle Ages. Thus, in a real sense there was little true corporate worship of all the people of God for well over a thousand years.

It was not until the rise of the liturgical movement in the recent decades of the twentieth century that Christian worship began once again to become truly important and relevant to Christianity. But working against centuries of tradition, the liturgical movement did not have the time or the support to do what it desired before Christian worship suddenly was being tested for immediate relevance. Despite adverse criticism, however, the liturgical movement proceeds with its task: primarily to restore corporate worship as essential to the Christian life; but now also to show its relevance to Christianity in a contemporary society.

It is no exaggeration that theology has rarely been helpful and often detrimental to Christian corporate worship. Developments in sacramental and eucharistic theology in the later patristic period, which became overemphasized in narrow definitions during the Middle Ages, primarily caused the decline of Christian worship. The elimination of the laity from real participation in worship and the emphasis upon the clergy as the center of worship clearly resulted from theological speculation about priesthood and sacraments, especially the sacrament of the Eucharist. The Protestant reformers became so engrossed in attacking and seeking to reform the same theological doctrines that they, too, never came to grips with worship itself. It is a remarkable fact that in Christian history theologians have offered doctrines of sacraments but not a doctrine of worship.

Worship as worship—whether it be a sacramental service, a preaching service, a choir office or whatever the form— must have theological grounding if it is to be recognized as central and meaningful to the Christian life. The time has come for the establishment of a real relationship between theology and worship. In fact the time has come for a theology of worship and not just a theology of sacraments. A preliminary step toward such a theology of worship was taken by the second Consultation on Church Union when it adopted the following: "[the] work of the Church is the place where grace as the pardoning and empowering act of God in Christ and faith as the response of man meet together, resulting in adoration, reconciliation, and loving obedience to him in worship, mission and witness to the world." (*Digest*, Vol. I-II, p. 47) In other words, when God's action in Christ and man's response of faith meet, then worship must be one of the chief results.

This preliminary approach to a theology of worship can be extremely helpful to Christian worship in its relation to contemporary society. Since in the last decades a highly complex nuclear-technological society has burst forth upon the world, it has become urgent that much of the Church's outlook and action be centered upon social and cultural matters. Unfortunately, though, some Christian leaders have concluded that if everything in the Church, worship included, does not have a one-to-one relationship with social and cultural action, then it is useless and irrelevant. A theology of worship will help to bring perspective and balance to the contemporary dilemma of the Church.

Such a theology would reveal that although worship and

Christian witness in the world are not to be separated, their ultimate concern lies in different directions. Such a theology would show that worship and social action are both primary results of man's response of faith to God's action in Christ. Such a theology would indicate that many of the materials and elements of worship—the body, the voice, the ear, food, water, song, and the proclamation of belief—are also the materials of social and cultural action.

Yet a theology of worship must also candidly declare that the primary object of Christian worship is God, whereas the primary object of Christian social and cultural action is man. Christian worship and Christian witness in the world must always be related, for both are results of faith. In a real sense each is dependent on and in need of the other if Christianity is to be effective in contemporary society; yet each must always differ from the other in its object. It is along these lines that a theology of worship is much needed in the Church today.

CHRISTIAN WORSHIP IN CONTEMPORARY SOCIETY: A LITURGICAL PROBLEM

A theology of worship will not of itself make Christian worship relevant to contemporary society without more creative reform in the ways of worship. No matter how constructive a theology of worship may be, if the forms of Christian worship remain bound to medieval and Reformation ideas, then worship will continue to appear irrelevant to contemporary society. It is fruitless, for example, for Anglicans to continue to revise the 1552 Prayer Book. The Cranmerian Prayer Books of the sixteenth century have ceased to be meaningful as models for liturgical revision. Worship in all churches needs much more radical change than the liturgical movement has yet accomplished or perhaps even suggested.

The greatest need is for worship to become genuinely corporate. All the people of God, especially the laity, must become fully involved in the worship of the Church, and priests and ministers must become less conspicuous in Christian liturgy. Full lay involvement means more than having a layman read the lessons at the morning service or the Epistle at Holy Communion; it means more than having men and women bring the bread and wine to the altar at the Communion. Certainly these have value, but at a given service they involve only a few lay people. And too often they become the beginning and the end of liturgical reform in the local church.

What is the best service or vehicle for full corporate worship? The Reformation Preaching Service is useless today for real corporate worship, chiefly because its center and context are the pulpit and the minister in a sixteenth- and seventeenth-century setting. Messages, speeches, and harangues constantly confront contemporary man from television, radio, motion pictures, newspapers, and magazines, as well as at his business and in his clubs and societies. He hardly needs a sermon, therefore, as the major part of his corporate worship of God. Yet the sermon has a key role in true corporate worship as will be noted.

The Anglican Morning Prayer service, from which many Protestant morning services have been adapted, is also inadequate for real corporate worship. Its context is the monastic chapel, whence its origin. When done daily by professional worshipers, such as monks or members of religious orders, seminarians, or cathedral choirs and clergy, Morning Prayer can be a meaningful vehicle of corporate worship for these professionals. The multitude of ordinary Christian laity are not, and should not be, professional worshipers; therefore, Morning Prayer will hardly involve them in corporate worship.

The one service which has potential for full Christian participation in worship is the Eucharist. (Here is meant the full Eucharist with Communion and not the truncated Mass, or Ante-Communion, regularly used in some European and American churches.) Although medieval developments and Reformation reactions have formed prejudices against the Communion in people's minds, from contemporary and historic viewpoints the Eucharist has the greatest possibility of all Christian forms for full corporate worship. Its context is a fellowship meal which involves everyone in the worship of God; in this service all the people of God have opportunity to offer their praise and thanksgiving to him. At the Eucharist all the people of God gather together around a common table; they participate in and receive the sacrament of unity; and they give expression to what the Church is seeking to witness to in social, cultural, and ecumenical action.

However, since the present service in most churches falls far short of involving all the people of God, the Eucharist is only potentially the best vehicle for corporate worship. Contemporary eucharistic services rarely allow the laity full opportunity to offer their praise and thanksgiving, nor do these services generate Christian witness in the world. The fault is not with the nature of eucharistic worship; the fault is with the kinds of eucharistic services that men have devised.

The order and content of Christian worship need careful study and experiment. Here we suggest three areas for immediate attention: the tone of the service, the language of worship, and the parts of the service which need greater emphasis. The tone of the service invariably excludes large numbers of lay people from sincere participation. Most services are full of pietism and solemnity; yet most laity are neither pietistic nor somber, nor should they be. Many parts of the service exist to convict the worshiper of his sin and unworthiness. He is bombarded with collects for purity, decalogues, summaries of the Law, exhortations, general confessions and absolutions, prayers of humble access, Agnus Deis, and the like.

Theologically these elements seem to negate the fact that Christ's incarnation and his redemptive acts of death and resurrection have reconciled God and man. Moreover, these numerous attempts to show man that he is evil and base become somewhat ridiculous as he roars off into space, perfects a successful polio vaccine, and invents incredible computers. Man does evil and is in need of repentance; this is basic to the Christian gospel. But general confessions and prayers for purity and worthiness are not going to accomplish real repentance. Eucharistic worship is not the place to win man's repentance, it is the place for men to offer together their praise and thanksgiving to God.

Another force which excludes many lay people from real participation in liturgy is the language of worship. Anglicans and Protestants formerly liked to criticize Roman Catholics because their worship was in Latin, a language few people understood well. Now that this problem has been rectified in much of Roman worship, perhaps Anglicans and Protestants will begin to look at the archaic language generally used in their own worship. The King James Version of the Bible and the various Anglican Prayer Books with their sixteenth- and seventeenth-century expressions are particular offenders in the language of liturgy.

Christian worship will continue to appear irrelevant or unreal for many lay people until liturgy is offered in contemporary language. When people speak, hear, and read one language in all their other activities of life, whether business, home, or recreation, it is folly to think that in worship they can set that language aside and really participate in a worship whose language is so very different. Furthermore, although the primary object of Christian worship is God, and the object of Christian witness in the world is man, these results of grace and faith should not be separated by language; yet so often the language of witness is very different from the words of worship. One of the crucial links between worship and everyday life which Christianity has often neglected is language.

When contemporary expression is introduced into worship, there are some who complain bitterly. Usually these are professional worshipers, clergy or laity, who have gained a personal apprehension of, or at least a personal attachment to, the archaic language. However, these people are really few in comparison to the numbers of men and women who are repelled by, and cannot find meaning in, the traditional language of worship. Moreover, it has happened that when worship is done in modern language, some people have been excited, even shocked, into participation because for the first time the language of worship is the language of life.

Constructive renewal of the tone and language of worship will inevitably demand great changes in the order and content of eucharistic services. It has already been suggested that the themes of penitence and worthiness are unnecessary if eucharistic worship is fully understood. The elimination of these elements will greatly shorten the services, and this in itself is another necessity in contemporary worship. The early church services were brief both because Sunday was a workday and people had to get to work, and because Christians lived under the threat of persecution and could not remain gathered together for long periods of time. Today the complexities and challenges of the ordinary layman's life are such that Christian worship is again in need of shorter services.

Throughout most of the history of Christian worship, the offertory and especially the Prayer of Consecration have been overemphasized in eucharistic worship. The time has come for them to be placed in a proper liturgical perspective. To be sure, both are essential to eucharistic worship, but they ought not to dominate the service. Contrary to the view of the reformers, who eliminated it, the offertory should remain in the service as an action to gather and to place the bread and wine on the altar. Although modern adaptations of early Christianity's offertory procession are helpful, the offertory needs nothing more than this kind of action; scriptural sentences or offertory prayers are unnecessary. Also contrary to the reformers' view, the Prayer of Consecration does not have to be reduced strictly to Jesus' words of institution. The historic theological themes reveal the liturgical and theological significance of the prayer, but certainly these themes can be expressed in far less verbiage than in the present Anglican, Roman, or Orthodox eucharistic prayers. That this can be done is shown in the eucharistic service of the Church of South India. The Prayer of Consecration in the South Indian liturgy not only retains most of the historic themes in shortened form but also involves congregational response and participation. It is not, therefore, just a lengthy prayer read exclusively by the priest. Hopefully this kind of forward-looking approach will be widely adopted as various churches revise their liturgy.

Four parts of the Eucharist which seem to need more careful attention and greater emphasis today are the reading of Scripture, the sermon, intercessory prayer, and the Communion. Scripture is basic to all forms of Christianity and has always been essential to Christian worship. Too often today, though, it seems to be a purposeless element in liturgy. It is frequently read in an archaic language, and the traditionally appointed lessons (Epistles and Gospels) often are far too obscure to provide meaning in contemporary worship. Yet Scripture can be translated into a modern idiom, and its message for today can begin to be revealed through newly appointed lessons. Scripture might also come alive in worship if clergy did more liturgical preaching on the lessons of the service.

Although the sermon should not dominate worship as in the Preaching Service, it has a significant role in eucharistic worship. Like language, the sermon is a crucial link between Christian worship and the Christian's witness in the world. The sermon is the place in worship for the proclamation of Christian responsibility in all of life; it is the place to interpret Christian witness in the world in relation to the doctrines and worship of the Church.

Perhaps more than the sermon, however, intercessory prayer is the place where worship and everyday life meet. The eucharistic intercessions have always been concerned with the people, the situations, and the events of contemporary life. Of course, many Christians do not realize this because in most services the intercessions are cast in obscure form and in archaic language. They are dominated by the clergy; the laity have no real participation in them. The Anglican Prayer for the Whole State of Christ's Church and the intercessions scattered about the Roman Prayer of Consecration well exemplify this point.

Intercessory prayer can be one of the main parts of the service in which all the people of God are fully involved. The intercessions should be cast in litany form, but not with the tedious repetition and obscure responses of traditional litanies. The key to relevant intercessory prayer is flexibility: the same intercessions need not be used at every eucharistic service; provision should be made for the use of particular names and situations; and this is a place where extemporaneous prayer ought to be permitted and even encouraged. Perhaps the laity would also participate more fully in the intercessions if this part of the service were done by members of the congregation and not by the ordained minister.

The greatest emphasis in the service should always be upon the act of Communion, the grand climax of eucharistic worship. This is when all the people of God gather together in corporate unity to receive the bread of life. All teaching and preaching about the Eucharist should center upon the Communion: its expression of Christian unity, its relation to Christian witness in all life, its sacramental benefits. All that is done in the eucharistic service points toward the climax of Holy Communion. The preparation of Scripture reading, sermon, and intercessory prayer followed by the act of offertory and a eucharistic prayer in which the congregation participates—all these elements lead to and culminate in the act of Communion. And except for song and ceremony, which in various degrees are necessary to Christian worship, these are all the elements necessary for Christian eucharistic worship.

How can such radical but necessary liturgical renewal be accomplished? Two complementary ways are suggested. First a stronger, more dedicated, and especially more creative liturgical movement must develop in all the churches of Christendom. Perhaps because it began as a revolutionary movement which needed widespread support if its purposes were to be accepted in the churches, the liturgical movement has sought its authorities and its security in the past. The extensive studies of biblical and patristic Christianity made in the last one hundred years proved a great boon to liturgical scholars. These studies revealed that worship in early Christianity was greatly different, more refreshing and vital than medieval, Reformation, and post-Reformation Christian worship. To date, therefore, many of the liturgical movement's programs have been based on worship in New Testament and early church Christianity. Some of the results of this program have been fruitful. However, if liturgical renewal is to become fully accepted throughout Christendom and also become a constructive element in modern Christianity, the liturgical movement must be more contemporarily creative. Worship in its historical perspective must always be a guide, and perhaps a corrective, for modern liturgical worship, but it cannot be the dominant factor.

Finally, liturgical renewal will give vitality and new life to Christian worship only if much more adventurous discussion and experiment take place in all churches. Such activity is greatly needed on the regional levels (presbyteries, districts, dioceses) of the churches. A greater imperative, however, is directed to the local congregations throughout Christendom where liturgical renewal is often unknown. Only when liturgical renewal reaches out to all the people of God will Christian worship regain its true meaning and centrality in Christian life.

General Bibliography

HISTORY AND THEOLOGY OF CHRISTIAN WORSHIP

Abba, Raymond, *Principles of Christian Worship*. New York: Oxford, 1957.

Addleshaw, G. W. O., and Etchells, Frederick, *The Architectural Setting of Anglican Worship*. London: Faber, 1948.

Addleshaw, G. W. O., *The High Church Tradition: A Study in the Liturgical Thought of the Seventeenth Century*. London: Faber, 1941.

Aulén, Gustaf, *Eucharist and Sacrifice*. Philadelphia: Muhlenberg, 1958.

Baumstark, Anton, *Comparative Liturgy*. London: Mowbray, 1958.

Biéler, André, *Architecture in Worship*. Edinburgh: Oliver & Boyd, 1965.

Bishop, Edmund, *Liturgica Historica*. Oxford: Clarendon, 1918.

Brightman, Frank E., *Liturgies, Eastern and Western*, Vol. I, *Eastern Liturgies*. Oxford: Clarendon, 1896.

—————— *The English Rite*. 2 vols. London: Rivingtons, 1915.

Brilioth, Yngve, *Eucharistic Faith and Practice*. London: SPCK, 1930.

Brook, Stella, *The Language of the Book of Common Prayer*. New York: Oxford, 1965.

Burnet, George B., *Holy Communion in the Reformed Church of Scotland: 1560-1960*. Edinburgh: Oliver & Boyd, 1960.

171

Cabasilas, Nicholas, *A Commentary on the Divine Liturgy*, trans. by Joan M. Hussey and Patricia A. McNulty. London: SPCK, 1st ed., 1960.

Casel, Odo, *The Mystery of Christian Worship*. Westminster, Md.: Newman, 1962.

Clark, Francis, *Eucharistic Sacrifice and the Reformation*. Westminster, Md.: Newman, 1960.

Cullmann, Oscar, *Early Christian Worship*. Chicago: Regnery, 1953.

Cullmann, Oscar, and Leenhardt, F. J., *Essays on the Lord's Supper*. Richmond: John Knox Press, 1958.

Cuming, Geoffrey J., ed., *The Durham Book: Being the First Draft of the Revision of the Book of Common Prayer in 1661*. London: Oxford, 1961.

Davies, Horton, *The Worship of the English Puritans*. Westminster: Dacre, 1948.

───── *Worship and Theology in England*. 5 vols. Princeton, N.J., Princeton, 1961-65.

Delling, Gerhard, *Worship in the New Testament*, trans. by Percy Scott. Philadelphia: Westminster, 1962.

Delorme, J., *The Eucharist in the New Testament*, trans. by E. M. Stewart. Baltimore: Helicon, 1964.

Dix, Gregory, *The Shape of the Liturgy*. Westminster: Dacre, 1945.

───── ed., *The Treatise on the Apostolic Tradition of St. Hippolytus of Rome*. New York: Macmillan, 1937.

Duchesne, Louis, *Christian Worship: Its Origin and Evolution*. 5th ed. London: SPCK, 1919.

Dugmore, Clifford W., *Eucharistic Doctrine in England from Hooker to Waterland*. London: SPCK, 1942.

───── *The Mass and the English Reformers*. London: Macmillan, 1958.

Dunlop, Colin, *Anglican Public Worship*. London: SCM, rev. ed., 1961.

Easton, Burton Scott, ed. *The Apostolic Tradition of Hippolytus*. New York: Cambridge, 1934.

Edwall, P., Hayman, E., and Maxwell, W., eds., *Ways of Worship*. New York: Harper, 1951.

Every, George, *Basic Liturgy: A Study in the Structure of the Eucharistic Prayer*. London: Faith, 1961.

Frere, Walter H., *The Anaphora, or the Great Eucharistic Prayer*. London: SPCK, 1938.

Gee, Henry, *The Elizabethan Prayer Book and Ornaments*. London: Macmillan, 1902.

Grisbrooke, Jardine, *Anglican Liturgies in the Seventeenth and Eighteenth Centuries*. London: SPCK, 1958.

Hageman, Howard G., *Pulpit and Table: Some Chapters in the History of Worship in the Reformed Churches*. Richmond: John Knox, 1962.

Hicks, Frederick C., *The Fullness of Sacrifice*. London: Macmillan, 1930.

Higgins, A. J., *The Lord's Supper in the New Testament*. Chicago: Regnery, 1952.

Hook, Norman, *The Eucharist in the New Testament*. London: Epworth, 1964.

Jeremias, Joachim, *The Eucharistic Words of Jesus*. New York: Macmillan, 1955.

Jungmann, Joseph A., *Public Worship*. London: Challoner, 1957.

―――― *The Early Liturgy to the Time of Gregory the Great*. Notre Dame, Ind.: Notre Dame, 1959.

―――― *The Eucharistic Prayer*. London: Challoner, 1962.

―――― *The Mass of the Roman Rite*. 2 vols. New York: Benziger, 1951.

Kidd, Beresford James, *The Later Medieval Doctrine of the Eucharistic Sacrifice*. London: SPCK, 1898.

King, A. A., *Liturgies of the Past*. Milwaukee: Bruce, 1959.

―――― *Liturgies of the Primatial Sees*. London: Longmans, 1957.

―――― *Liturgies of the Religious Orders*. London: Longmans, 1955.

Klauser, Theodor, *The Western Liturgy Today,* trans. by F. L. Cross. Westminster, Md.: Canterbury, 1963.

Ladd, William Palmer, *Prayer Book Interleaves.* New York: Seabury, 1957.
Legg, John Wickham, ed., *Cranmer's Liturgical Projects.* London: Harrison, 1915.
Lietzmann, Hans, *Mass and the Lord's Supper.* Leiden: Brill, 1953.
Lowther-Clarke, W. K., and Harris, Charles, eds., *Liturgy and Worship.* London: SPCK, 1932.

MacLeod, Donald, *Presbyterian Worship: Its Meaning and Method.* Richmond, Va.: John Knox, 1965.
Maxwell, William D., *An Outline of Christian Worship: Its Development and Forms.* London: Oxford, 1936.
Michell, Gilbert A., *Landmarks in Liturgy.* London: Darton, 1961.
Micklem, Nathaniel, *Christian Worship.* Oxford: Clarendon, 1936.
Minchin, Basil, *Covenant and Sacrifice.* London: Longmans, 1958.
Moule, C. F. D., *Worship in the New Testament.* Richmond, Va.: John Knox, 1961.

Norman, James Roy, *Handbook to the Christian Liturgy.* London: SPCK, 1944.
Norris, Herbert, *Church Vestments: Their Origin and Development.* New York: Dutton, 1950.

Oesterley, W. O. E., *The Jewish Background of Christian Worship.* Oxford: Clarendon, 1925.

Parsch, Pius, *The Liturgy of the Mass.* 3rd ed., St. Louis: Herder, 1957.
Parsons, Edward L., and Jones, Bayard H., *The American Prayer Book: Its Origins and Principles.* New York: Scribners, 1937.
Peaston, Alexander E., *The Prayer Book Reform Movement in the Eighteenth Century.* Oxford: Blackwell, 1940.

—— *The Prayer Book Tradition in the Free Churches.* Naperville, Ill.: Allenson, 1964.

Porter, H. Boone, *The Day of Light: The Biblical and Liturgical Meaning of Sunday.* New York: Seabury, 1960.

Porter, William S., *The Gallican Rite.* London: Mowbray, 1958.

Proctor, Francis, and Frere, Walter H., *A New History of the Book of Common Prayer.* London: Macmillan, rev. ed., 1905.

Ramsey, Arthur Michael, et al. *The English Prayer Book: 1549-1662.* London: SPCK, 1963.

Reed, Luther D., *The Lutheran Liturgy.* Philadelphia: Muhlenberg, 1947.

Richardson, Cyril C., *Zwingli and Cranmer on the Eucharist.* Evanston, Ill.: Seabury-Western Theological Seminary, 1949.

Salaville, Sévérien, *An Introduction to the Study of Eastern Liturgies.* London: Sands, 1938.

Schmemann, Alexander, *Introduction to Liturgical Theology.* Clayton, Wis.: American Orthodox Press, 1965.

Shepherd, Massey H., *At All Times and in All Places.* New York: Seabury, rev. ed., 1953.

—— *The Oxford American Prayer Book Commentary.* New York: Oxford, 1950.

—— *The Paschal Liturgy and the Apocalypse.* Richmond, Va.: John Knox, 1960.

—— *The Worship of the Church.* New York: Seabury, 1953.

Srawley, James Herbert, *The Early History of the Liturgy.* 2nd ed., Cambridge, 1947.

Stone, Darwell, *A History of the Doctrine of the Holy Eucharist.* 2 vols. London: Longmans, 1909.

Streng, W., *Toward Meaning in Worship: An Introduction to the Lutheran Liturgy.* Minneapolis: Augsburg, 1964.

Swete, H. B., *Services and Service Books Before the Reformation.* London: SPCK, 1896.

Thompson, Bard, ed., *Liturgies of the Western Church*. Cleveland: World, 1962.

Thurian, Max, *The Eucharistic Memorial*. 2 vols. Richmond, Va.: John Knox, 1960.

Underhill, Evelyn, *Worship*. New York: Harper, 1937.

Van Dijk, S. J. P., *Sources of the Modern Roman Liturgy*. 2 vols. Leiden: Brill, 1963.

West, R. C., *Western Liturgies*. London: SPCK, 1938.

Wigan, Bernard, ed., *The Liturgy in English*. New York: Oxford, 1962.

Willis, Geoffrey G., *Essays in Early Roman Liturgy*. London: SPCK, 1964.

Wordsworth, John, *Bishop Sarapion's Prayer Book*. London: SPCK, 1899.

CONTEMPORARY LITURGICAL RENEWAL AND THE LITURGICAL MOVEMENT

Benoit, Jean Daniel, *Liturgical Renewal: Studies in Catholic and Protestant Developments on the Continent*, trans. by Edwin Hudson. London: SCM, 1958.

Bouyer, Louis, *Liturgical Piety*. Notre Dame, Ind.: Notre Dame, 1954.

———— *The Liturgy Revived: A Doctrinal Commentary of the Conciliar Constitution on the Liturgy*. Notre Dame, Ind.: Notre Dame, 1964.

Browne, R. E. C., *The Ministry of the Word*. London: SCM, 1958.

Cellier, Frank, ed., *Liturgy Is Mission*. New York: Seabury, 1964.

Church of South India, *Book of Common Worship*. London: Oxford, 1963.

Clark, Neville, *Call to Worship*. London: SCM, 1960.

Cope, G. F., Davies, J. G., and Tytler, D. A., *An Experimental Liturgy*. Richmond, Va.: John Knox, 1958.

Daniélou, Jean, *The Bible and the Liturgy*. Notre Dame, Ind.:
    Notre Dame, 1956.
Diekmann, Godfrey, *Come, Let Us Worship*. Baltimore: Helicon,
    1961.

Garrett, Thomas S., *Worship in the Church of South India*. Rich-
    mond: John Knox, 1958.
Guardini, Romano, *The Spirit of the Liturgy*. London: Sheed &
    Ward, 1935.

Hebert, A. G., *Liturgy and Society*. London: Faber, 1935.
—— ed., *The Parish Communion*. London: SPCK, 1937.
Hovda, Robert, ed., *Sunday Morning Crisis: Renewal in Catholic
    Worship*. Baltimore: Helicon, 1963.

James, E., *The Roots of the Liturgy*. London: Prism Pamphlets,
    1962.
Jasper, Ronald C. D., ed., *The Renewal of Worship*. London:
    Oxford, 1965.

King, James W., *The Liturgy and the Laity*. Westminster, Md.:
    Newman, 1963.
Koenker, Ernest, *The Liturgical Renaissance in the Roman Catho-
    lic Church*. Chicago: University of Chicago, 1954.

Lockett, William, ed., *The Modern Architectural Setting of the
    Liturgy*. London: SPCK, 1964.

McManus, Frederick, *The Revival of Liturgy*. New York: Herder,
    1963.
Martin, John T., *Christ Our Passover: The Liturgical Observance
    of Holy Week*. London: SCM, 1958.
Minchin, Basil, *Every Man in His Ministry*. London: Darton,
    1960.

Naylor, Charles Basil, *Why Prayer Book Revision at All?* Lon-
    don: Church Information Office, 1964.

Nicholls, William, *Jacob's Ladder: The Meaning of Worship.*
    Richmond: John Knox, 1958.

Paton, David M., ed., *The Parish Communion Today.* London,
    SPCK, 1962.
Prayer Book Studies. 17 vols. New York: Church Pension Fund,
    1950-.

Robinson, John A. T., *Liturgy Coming to Life.* Philadelphia:
    Westminster, 1964.

Shands, A. R., *The Liturgical Movement and the Local Church.*
    London: SCM, rev. ed., 1965.
Shepherd, Massey H., *Liturgy and Education.* New York: Sea-
    bury, 1965.
———— ed., *The Eucharist and Liturgical Renewal.* New York:
    Oxford, 1960.
———— ed., *The Liturgical Renewal of the Church.* New York:
    Oxford, 1960.
———— *The Living Liturgy.* New York: Oxford, 1946.
———— *The Reform of Liturgical Worship.* New York: Oxford,
    1961.
———— ed., *Worship in Scripture and Tradition.* New York: Ox-
    ford, 1963.
Srawley, James Herbert, *The Liturgical Movement: Its Origin and
    Growth.* London: Mowbray, 1954.

Taylor, Michael J., *The Protestant Liturgical Renewal: A Catholic
    Viewpoint.* Westminster, Md.: Newman, 1963.

Warren, Max, ed., *A Conversation About the Holy Communion.*
    London: SCM, 1964.
Winward, Stephen F., *The Reformation of Our Worship.* Rich-
    mond, Va.: John Knox, 1965.

Yarnold, G. D., *The Bread Which We Break.* New York: Oxford,
    1964.

Index